DIGITAL, DIVERSE & DIVIDED

DIGITAL, DIVERSE & DIVIDED

How to Talk to Racists, Compete with Robots, and Overcome Polarization

DAVID LIVERMORE

BK®

Berrett–Koehler Publishers, Inc.

Berrett-Koehler Publishers, Inc.
1333 Broadway, Suite 1000
Oakland, CA 94612-1921
Tel: (510) 817-2277 | Fax: (510) 817-2278
www.bkconnection.com

ORDERING INFORMATION
QUANTITY SALES. Special discounts are available on quantity purchases by corporations, associations, and others. For details, contact the "Special Sales Department" at the Berrett-Koehler address above.
INDIVIDUAL SALES. Berrett-Koehler publications are available through most bookstores. They can also be ordered directly from Berrett-Koehler: Tel: (800) 929-2929; Fax: (802) 864-7626; www.bkconnection.com.
ORDERS FOR COLLEGE TEXTBOOK / COURSE ADOPTION USE. Please contact Berrett-Koehler: Tel: (800) 929-2929; Fax: (802) 864-7626.

Distributed to the US trade and internationally by Penguin Random House Publisher Services.

Printed in Canada

Berrett-Koehler books are printed on long-lasting acid-free paper. When it is available, we choose paper that has been manufactured by environmentally responsible processes. These may include using trees grown in sustainable forests, incorporating recycled paper, minimizing chlorine in bleaching, or recycling the energy produced at the paper mill.

LIBRARY OF CONGRESS CATALOGING-IN-PUBLICATION DATA
Names: Livermore, David A., 1967– author.
Title: Digital, diverse & divided : how to talk to racists, compete with robots, and overcome polarization / by David Livermore, PhD.
Other titles: Digital, diverse and divided
Description: First edition. | Oakland, CA : Berrett-Koehler Publishers, [2022] | Includes bibliographical references and index.
Identifiers: LCCN 2022002042 (print) | LCCN 2022002043 (ebook) | ISBN 9781523000920 (hardcover ; alk. paper) | ISBN 9781523000937 (pdf) | ISBN 9781523000944 (epub)
Subjects: LCSH: Toleration. | Social conflict. | Cultural intelligence. | Intercultural communication.
Classification: LCC HM1271 .L498 2022 (print) | LCC HM1271 (ebook) | DDC 179/.9—dc23/eng/20220427
LC record available at https://lccn.loc.gov/2022002042
LC ebook record available at https://lccn.loc.gov/2022002043

FIRST EDITION
29 28 27 26 25 24 23 22 ◊ 10 9 8 7 6 5 4 3 2 1

Book producer and text designer: BookMatters
Cover designer: Adam Johnson

For Linda, Emily, and Grace.
You're the center of my world.

People fail to get along because they fear each other; they fear each other because they don't know each other; they don't know each other because they have not communicated with each other.

—MARTIN LUTHER KING JR.

CONTENTS

	Prologue	1
PART I	**Why Can't We All Just Get Along?**	5
ONE	Closer Than We Appear	7
TWO	Yet We're So Different	19
THREE	And Then There's You	29
PART II	**Building a More Culturally Intelligent World**	39
FOUR	What's Your CQ?	41
FIVE	How to Navigate Polarizing Conversations	55
SIX	How to Compete with Robots	69
PART III	**CQ Solutions for Polarized Worlds**	85
SEVEN	Place	87
EIGHT	Race	101

NINE Pronouns 119
TEN G/god/s 135
ELEVEN Politics 151
Epilogue 165

Questions for Reflection and Discussion 169
Notes 173
Acknowledgments 183
Index 187
About the Author 195

PROLOGUE

It was ten minutes before I was going to start teaching a weeklong executive MBA class. Forty leaders from around the world were in Singapore for my course on cultural intelligence. As I walked around the room to informally introduce myself, I greeted an enormously tall Norwegian executive who was leaning against the back wall. After reluctantly shaking my hand, he said, "To be clear, I'm only here because this is required. I've been doing international business for twenty years, and it has nothing to do with all this politically correct bullshit about cultural intelligence. I don't care what's between someone's legs or the color of their skin. They just need to do their job. But if you can keep me from suing our Chinese subcontractors by the end of the week, maybe I'll change my mind."

Game on! This executive assumed I'd spend the week teaching things he had heard countless times before—self-awareness, cultural sensitivity, and learning about cultural differences. But I had a different strategy in mind. Within the first hour, I asked the leaders to identify a problem in their organizations that requires different groups working together. I promised the tools to constructively address the problem with the problem itself being a key catalyst for overcoming the divides.

I want to help you do the same thing. This book is about how to get along with people who are different. It sounds about as simple as you can get. It's the first thing we're taught in kindergarten, and it's a standing topic at corporate off-site retreats and international diplomacy efforts. Yet we do it so poorly. I'm convinced that polarization is the number-one issue facing our world today. We encounter it at every turn. Social media used to be a place to reconnect with long lost friends. Now it's become a platform to spout political views and unfollow anyone who disagrees. Diversity programs were supposed to increase inclusion and belonging. Instead, they seem to exhaust everyone, including the individuals leading them. And families and friendships are being destroyed because we can't agree on issues of race, religion, and politics.

Now, based on research published in hundreds of peer-reviewed journals, cultural intelligence offers a better way forward. With cultural intelligence we have the tools to relate and work together without losing ourselves in the process. Cultural intelligence, or CQ®, is rooted in decades of research across 150 countries and it's defined as the *capability to relate and work effectively with people who have different backgrounds*—nationality, ethnicity, gender, religion, politics, and more. CQ provides a practical, evidence-based approach for making sense of our differences and learning how to bridge our divides without forcing everyone to conform to the same thinking and behavior.

I've had the privilege of being part of the cultural intelligence research from the beginning. I wrote this book to apply these findings to the relationships that matter most to us—personally and professionally. You'll hear an abundance of stories, some of which stem from my own experiences; most come from qualitative data I've collected over the past twenty-five years. To protect confidentiality, I've changed the names, but the remaining details are as told to me.

I want to emphasize that this is an opt-in experience. If you're repeatedly on the receiving end of discrimination and bigotry, I make no assumptions about whether you should pursue talking to people who disrespect you. There's an emotional weight and fatigue that comes with doing this work, especially for those who are marginalized. Talking about the long history of racism or explaining why a sexist comment isn't funny can stir up all kinds of pain and anger. But for those seeking help to navigate polarized situations, I want to offer guidance and hope.

As a straight, white, middle-aged guy, I acknowledge that there are aspects of our polarized world that are mostly theoretical to me. I rarely experience the direct impact of discrimination and bias, and I've wrestled with whether it's my place to write a book about it. But the research on cultural intelligence is increasingly applicable to the differences polarizing us all across the world, so I offer these findings to be part of the solution. It also doesn't seem right to put all the responsibility on those who are consistently marginalized. We all have a part to play in building a more culturally intelligent world; I do so with an understanding that my perspective has limitations.

Part I of the book lays the foundation for understanding our digital, diverse, and divided world. By beginning with how we're alike and how we're different, we have a critical starting point for tackling polarization. Part II shows how to apply cultural intelligence to everyday life, both personally and professionally. And in Part III we encounter five worlds that profoundly shape the way we feel about polarizing issues like immigration, gender fluidity, racism, Covid-19, and whatever other culture wars we encounter. Place, race, gender, faith, and politics aren't the only worlds that divide us, but they're among the most critical. Cultivating cultural intelligence can help.

By the end of my weeklong course on cultural intelligence, the Norwegian executive decided to delay suing his Chinese contractors. For me, that was a good start. Six months later, he sent me an email to say they had worked through their differences and were forming a joint venture. Tackling polarization isn't easy, but we can do it. So let's get to it.

PART I

Why Can't We All Just Get Along?

We're living in an age of massive global disruption that includes two major forces—technological and sociological change. Technologically, social media and artificial intelligence are changing the way people think, live, and relate. Sociologically, our increased interconnectivity with people across the globe exposes us to perspectives and people from all walks of life.

We're in a new frontier. We all do intercultural work now. Whether it's attending Zoom meetings all hours of the day, scrolling through social media, or waking up to terse emails from across the world, encountering difference is a reality for all of us, all the time. We're so much alike, and yet so very different. That's the problem, but it's also the solution. Let's begin there, with the goal of finding unity in our different ways of being human.

ONE

Closer Than We Appear

I've been researching and writing about cultural intelligence for twenty-five years. But a taxi driver summed up the essence of cultural intelligence for me in one statement: "You are not American, and I am not Pakistani. Those are just government labels. We are brothers; and if we stick together, we'll be okay."

His words really struck me. I know. It sounds rather Pollyannish. But context is everything. Just minutes before, I had walked through the lobby of my Dubai hotel where a group was gathered around a TV watching the first presidential debate between Donald Trump and Joe Biden. The group burst out laughing as Trump taunted Biden, saying, "Every time you see him, he's got a mask. He could be speaking two hundred feet away…and he shows up with the biggest mask I've ever seen." The group was equally amused when Biden called the sitting president a clown and said, "Will you shut up man?"[1]

I scurried by hoping no one would "mistake" me as an American. We were in the worst pandemic in a hundred years and the two guys vying for the top job in the US were clowning around calling each other names. When I jumped in a taxi a few minutes later, I felt a bit reluctant to answer my driver's question, "Where are you from?" After I eventually told him I'm from the US, I jokingly said, "But don't hold that against me," which prompted his response: "We are brothers."

We had a fascinating conversation, as so often happens with taxi drivers. He told me his favorite thing to do on the weekend is to watch sports with a group of Indians and Pakistanis, who are supposed to hate each other, but instead consider each other best of friends in their home away from home. I was so struck by our conversation that I shared an excerpt on social media. People immediately responded with likes, hearts, and shares. And the enthusiastic affirmations came from both extremes of the liberal-conservative divide.

It doesn't take much to tap our desire to connect as humans. So why does it feel like polarization is worse than ever? Before we can address the differences that divide us, we need to see how much we're alike. Our shared humanity is the antidote to hate. Rest easy, this isn't going to be an overly simplistic "we're all the same" kumbaya treatise. But the journey toward cultural intelligence begins with seeing one another's humanity.

Same DNA

Ahmet and Jonas grew up next door to each other in the 1940s and 1950s. They lived in Potamia, a farming village just outside Nicosia, Cyprus. They did everything together—playing in their adjoining yards, walking to school, and working for a nearby farmer. Ahmet is Muslim and Jonas is Christian, typical of their respective Turkish and Greek Cypriot families. Ahmet's mother routinely shared extra loaves of the special bread she baked for Muslim holidays with Jonas's family. Jonas's mother reciprocated during Greek Orthodox celebrations. This was typical life for many Cypriots prior to 1974. But suddenly the island that had been a nexus of East and West was divided by a buffer zone stretching more than a hundred miles across the country. The birthplace of Aphrodite, the island of love, sunny beaches, and charming villages became a place guarded by the United Nations. And friendships like Ahmet's and Jonas's were ripped apart.

We all come from Africa—Ahmet, Jonas, you, and me. And for $99, you can find out how much African descent remains in your DNA. Ancestry tests have soared in popularity with people discovering surprising links and tracking down unknown relatives across the world. The success of these tests is rooted in the tacit assumption that our DNA can sort us into five races: African, European, Asian, Oceanic, and Native American. While the ancestry industry taps our curiosity about where we're from, there's no scientific evidence that race is a biological reality. What the research actually tells us is that the basic DNA of all human beings—Black, Indigenous, white, immigrant—is the same.

The decisive scientific study that put a nail in the coffin of race was the Human Genome Project (HGP), a massive project led by an international team of researchers that attempted to sequence and map all the genes of humanity. The result was detailed information—about three billion letters of genetic code—that essentially gave us the instructions for how a human being is made and a map for how we function.[2]

The completion of the HGP garnered worldwide attention. Perhaps the most striking finding was that our DNA is 99.9 percent the same. Men, women, short, tall, blonde, brunette, tongue-curlers, color-blind—we all share an almost identical sequence of nucleotides in our DNA.[3] Upon completion of the Human Genome Project, President Bill Clinton stood in the East Room at the White House and declared: "I believe one of the great truths to emerge from this triumphant expedition inside the human genome is that in genetic terms, all human beings, regardless of race, are more than 99.9 percent the same.... The most important fact of life on this earth is our common humanity."[4]

The Human Genome Project stood in contrast to "science" that allegedly proved racial differences. In the 1700s, Swedish physician and taxonomist Carl Linnaeus was at the forefront of creating four utterly reprehensible and indefensible biological categories:

> *Europaeus albus* (European): White, serious, and strong people with flowing blonde hair and blue eyes. Linnaeus described this group as active, smart, and inventive.
>
> *Asiaticus fuscus* (Asian): Yellow, melancholy, and greedy people with black hair and dark eyes. They were classified as severe, haughty, and driven by desire.
>
> *Americanus rubescens* (Native American): Red, ill-tempered, and subjugated with black, straight, thick hair, wide nostrils, a harsh face, and a scanty beard. Linnaeus described them as obstinate, content, and free.
>
> *Africanus niger* (African Black): Black, passive, and lazy with kinky hair, silky skin, a flat nose, and thick lips. They were identified as crafty, slow, and foolish. Linnaeus speculated they might not be fully human.[5]

Linnaeus's reprehensible categories gave colonists just the rationalization they needed to prove that some people are more human than others. When the Dutch first colonized Africa in the seventeenth century, they referred to the locals as animals, who on occasion needed to be shot and eaten. Political leaders used this shoddy science to defend saying things like: "[These people] are not fit to live among us. They are animals, and they behave like animals.... Inarticulate sounds pour out of their bestial skulls."[6] The problem is, that quote is from Zsolt Bayer, a contemporary politician in Hungary who consistently alerts Hungarians to the "ills" of the Romani people. Three centuries after Linnaeus's ludicrous "findings," we're still dehumanizing people from different worlds.

Ahmet left Cyprus to attend university in Turkey, where he stayed for many years. He eventually came back to Cyprus. His family was now living in a modest home in a Turkish Cypriot village on the far east side of the country. Ahmet rented a small flat on the Turkish side of Nicosia, less than a mile from where Jonas lived with his wife and children, but the boyhood friends were separated by a border that neither of them was permitted to cross. Ahmet attempted to contact Jonas but never received a reply. He felt invisible in his own country and as if he was the enemy. He wondered if his childhood soulmate agreed with what online newspapers repeatedly wrote about Turk Cypriots—"backward, nonentities" who must not be allowed to hold the country back.

Two men who started out as childhood friends had their lives ripped apart. There's very little about us that's different biologically. Yet we so easily sort ourselves into us-versus-them groups.

Human Universals

When I was working on my PhD, I was interested in discovering similarities in how people from different cultures learn. My adviser immediately corrected me: "The real discoveries are found in the *differences*, not the similarities." She said: "You need to remove that objective from your proposal. The committee will never approve something so superficial." As a social scientist, I was trained to focus on cultural *differences*. Any emphasis on similarities and common themes was considered superficial and missing the point.

Diversity experts are known for saying, "Break the golden rule. *Don't* treat others the way *you* want to be treated. Treat others the way *they* want to be treated." Differences are the holy grail of sociology and anthropology. Yet I sometimes wonder if our overemphasis on differences has gone too far. And I'm not alone. Kimberlé Crenshaw, the originator of the enormously useful concept of intersectionality, worries that her work has been misinterpreted and used to divide people into more and more subgroups while missing the point of what she was after. Intersectionality highlights the inadequacy of broad descriptions like African American or female by showing that we all have a mosaic of identities. But Crenshaw says her work has been taken too far and become "identity politics on steroids."[7]

We're right to caution against group blindness (e.g., "I don't see color"), but we seem to have lost the value of seeing our shared humanity. There's so much about us as humans that we have in common. *The MIT Encyclopedia of Cognitive Sciences* lists hundreds of characteristics that anthropologist Donald Brown has cataloged as human universals. These are features shared across every nationality, race, gender, faith, and political group. Maybe our differences have been overplayed.

Human universals include core characteristics like our shared need for food and rest or the ubiquitous presence of love and romance across all cultures, but we also share universal quirks. We dance, marry, style our hair, use weapons, and adorn our bodies with jewelry and tattoos. People from nearly every race, place, and faith do these things. But animals don't. Your dog doesn't put on makeup.[8]

As a shameless foodie, I'm particularly interested in Brown's analysis of our universal connection to food. I've always thought about food as a profound difference between cultures—how we eat, when we eat, and what we eat. But while other animals simply capture their food and eat it, humans season it, think about what to pair with it, and cook it. And not only are we universally epicurean in how we prepare our food, we make eating an event, sitting down to share a meal at certain times of the day—a uniquely human phenomenon.[9]

Another fascinating universal on Brown's list is gossip. Whether I'm running around the lake by my house, sitting in an airport overseas, or working from a coffee shop, I consistently hear people around me gossiping about coworkers, family, and friends. Oxford researcher Robin Dunbar says our universal tendency to gossip isn't so much about the person being talked about; it's about the bonds created by gossiping. A shared annoyance brings people together. Complaining to a fellow passenger about the inept airline, texting a friend about the annoying group chat, or complaining to a colleague about incompetent leadership creates a bond around shared irritations. Many of us think that peace, love, and cooperation bring us together. But gossip and complaining might do it better.[10]

There are hundreds more human universals. A human universal doesn't mean no group or individual ever contradicts it, but these are characteristics that nearly everyone has in common regardless of ethnicity, gender, sexual orientation, age, or any other dimension of identity. We're the only creatures that have sex in private. We share a fear of snakes. We process information logically, marry each other, develop grammar and syntax, and create visual arts.

Stop and think about a group that feels utterly foreign to you. It might be a tribal group in the Southern Hemisphere, or it may just as easily be people in your own community who couldn't view the world more differently than you. List what you have in common with these individuals. I guarantee you'll discover some commonalities. Write these down as the first step in reframing the way you see your Other.

I met Ahmet when we were both visiting London. He and I come from very different worlds. When we sat down together at a café, I wondered if I'd be able to establish rapport with someone twenty-five years my senior who has lived most of his adult life as a second-class citizen in his own country. He insisted on buying my coffee and immediately asked about my wife and kids. We both have daughters, which gave us an instant bond. His bulging blue eyes welled up as he shared his enormous regret for the years he stopped talking to one of his girls because she refused to "stop being gay." There we sat, two men from entirely different worlds, yet as two fathers we understood the joy and pain we feel for our kids.

Emotions are another universal we all share. But our cultures teach us to express emotions differently, something that is exceptionally difficult to decode online. Parents teach children the appropriate emotional response for various occasions, which is reinforced at school, through the media, and with peers.

A few years ago, I had the misfortune of seeing a Chinese man jump from a building in Shanghai to his death below. My heart stopped. *What could possibly lead this guy to such immense despair?* But what happened next alarmed me almost as much as the suicide. Several people gathered around the body, looking at each other and quietly giggling. I was so unnerved by the response. After reflecting on it further, I realized that the giggling may well have been a way for the onlookers to disguise their horror. Fake laughter and giggles are a common response to nervousness and discomfort among some Asian cultures.

Our various cultures teach us how to manage our feelings, which can lead us to wrongly interpret others' emotional reactions. But at our core, we all experience the same set of emotions, a bond that offers us a way to reach across the polarizing divides.

Degrees of Humanity

In 2010, Ahmet made his first trek across the buffer zone in Nicosia. It had been decades since he had traveled to the other side of the capital. He was stunned as he walked along the chic promenade filled with brand names he had seen on the streets of Istanbul and London. Here they were, just a mile from his home. Ahmet heard that Jonas was a professor at a university in town. He recently came across an online article quoting Jonas as saying, "Any true Muslim is a jihadist." Ahmet couldn't believe Jonas would say such things. This was not the gentle kid who joined Ahmet's family for iftar, the evening meal eaten together during Ramadan. But war and politics change people. It would be understandable if Ahmet had opted out of interacting with Jonas. It's not on the oppressed and marginalized to make the first move to reach across the divide. The emotional labor and disproportionate impact of polarization on marginalized groups is something we will repeatedly consider throughout the book. But Ahmet was determined to pursue contact with Jonas.

The two men, now in their sixties, eventually met for coffee. They started by awkwardly catching up on the past forty-five years and avoided any discussion of politics. They reminisced about a girl they both had a crush on when they were teenagers. This was the first of many coffees, text messages, and email exchanges, which eventually led the men to discuss religion and politics. They traveled back to their neighborhood in Potamia together. Jonas was not the man he appeared to be when only reading his edited comments in click-bait news articles. Much of Jonas's career had been spent striving for reconciliation among fellow Cypriots. The quotation Ahmet read had been printed out of context, as so often happens in the digital world. What Jonas actually said was, "While some say *any true Muslim is a jihadist*, we all know that to be completely untrue." Many news and social media companies profit by dividing us. But we have the power to stop it by forging relationships with the other side. Ahmet and Jonas began to spend time together weekly and rekindled their childhood bond. They eventually invited their families and other friends to join them.

Discrimination is rooted in believing that some people are less human than others. The Nazis called Jews "rats," the Hutus called Tutsis "cockroaches," and the US Founding Fathers decided enslaved Black people counted as three-fifths of a person. Labels that dehumanize are continually broadcast into our minds: crazy libs, country bumpkins, homophobes, and deplorables. Sean Hannity, one of the most conservative newscasters in mainstream media, opened his February 5, 2020, show on Fox News with big red letters on the screen that read: "Three Year Tantrum." His opening monologue started with this: "The three-year tantrum led by the Schumer Schiff Sham is over. The bitter do-nothing Democrats have been defeated and President Trump is acquitted."[11] Meanwhile, MSNBC newscaster Rachel Maddow says that the Republican party has become a "fringe, violent, extremist criminal movement." Her underlying message is, if you defend Trump, you're a violent extremist. Rather than news, we get a lot of personal commentary that pits Americans against each other, slowly but steadily questioning the humanity of the other side.

What happens when a society views some members as lower life forms? The result is not only war but the justification of suicide bombings and soldiers killing children. Dehumanization is a mental trick that gives us permission to mistreat others. Ntou Kteily, a Lebanese American psychologist, is hopeful, however. His research shows that our brains can be rewired to forge trust and understanding through contact and collaborative problem-solving.[12] This is what Ahmet and Jonas began to experience together. They rediscovered their childhood friendship and applied their renewed understanding to other Cypriots.

Reclaiming our shared humanity is as simple as slowing down long enough to see each other beneath the surface of polarizing issues. When you see a neighbor displaying a flag that rubs you the wrong way, stop to think beyond the symbol to consider who they really are. *What keeps them awake at night? Why might they support a cause that is so offensive to me?* You don't have to agree with someone to openly consider what brought them to the perspectives they have. When you see an Internet meme that mocks people who have a different opinion about immigration or vaccines, stop and think about whether resharing it does anything to make things better. Consider how someone you love might be hurt by this caricature and whether the "likes" and laughs it gets from others are worth it.

Same but Different

One of my favorite pastimes is to watch people. I look at a family of five riding by on a motorcycle in Phnom Penh and I wonder where they are going, how they get along, and what their lives are like. I drive by wide-open farms across rural America and wonder what stories exist behind the people driving the tractors across the sprawling fields. And I scroll through photos on social media and wonder what was really going on for the people in a picture.

We're all so different—the foods we like, the things we find funny, the ways we communicate, and the things that upset us. Yet we're all so much the same. We all eat and sleep, seek meaning and purpose in life, care for our kids, and enjoy a little bit of gossip. It sounds so simple. Our biological core is 99.9 percent the same. So why is it so incredibly hard for us to get along?

TWO

Yet We're So Different

Simon is a middle-class American teenager who, after eighteen years of life in a Milwaukee suburb, goes away to college. Madison, Wisconsin, is less than two hours away, but it's a world apart from home. Simon loves his parents, but he's intoxicated by his newfound freedom as a college student. He can come and go as he pleases, stay up as late as he wants, and dress however he likes with no questions asked. In reality, however, Simon has simply signed up for life with a new list of constraints and expectations.

It's not so much the new rules at college as it is the unspoken norms. Simon meets peers who size up whether he's cool enough to hang out with. Faculty and administrators indoctrinate him with messages about diversity, taking responsibility, and standing apart so he can get a job when he graduates. His female peers in the pre-med program are applauded for breaking stereotypes, but he wonders if it would be equally celebrated if he switched his major to nursing. The jarring experience of this new world makes the prospect of Greek life extremely inviting.*

* "Greek life" is a significant part of many US universities. It consists of social organizations overseen by national charters, with young men belonging to fraternities and young women to sororities. One university may have dozens of fraternities and sororities, each of which offers housing (e.g., a frat house) that is only available to their group members.

If Simon joins a fraternity, he instantly has a place where he belongs. Getting inducted into Tau Kappa Epsilon doesn't come easily, but once he's a member, Simon has a new in-group that is formed in large part by pitting itself against the frat house across the street. Ironically, pretty much all the houses along "Frat Row" live by the same rules, but part of being "in" is positioning yourselves against other groups, or what we often refer to as the out-group. Frat life includes hooking up with girls and getting high-fives from your bros. If girls aren't your thing, there's a special fraternity for you, but it's probably not this one. As one frat guy says: "It's not really about the girls. It's about the praise of your brothers, about your brothers knowing you hooked up with this girl."[1]

Simon, like hundreds of people I've interviewed over the past twenty-five years, demonstrates the power of in-groups to shape who we are and how we relate with people who are different. Simon can decide to remain celibate and avoid the drinking games at school, but it's not going to be easy. His thinking, values, and choices are profoundly shaped by the people he spends time with, and the same is true for you and me. Is it any surprise that you see the same kind of cars, yard furniture, and architectural styles from one neighborhood to the next?

Several studies show that most people vacation at the same places as their friends, share a similar diet, vote similarly, and have similar beliefs. Without even trying, we become conformists to the people we spend time with. We learn what's "normal" through the figured worlds of which we're part. "Figured worlds" is a concept developed by anthropologist Dorothy Holland to explain the power of our social environments to shape the way we see ourselves and others. These are the imaginary realms that form us and, in turn, we reform them. They are the context in which we live life, and they write the scripts we live. What we think, how we behave, and the choices we make are profoundly shaped by our figured worlds.[2] We're each part of many figured worlds, but five of the most polarizing worlds stem from the places we call home, the race/s with which we identify, and our gender, faith, and political identities.

The Human Genome Project proved we're one human race. Simon has pretty much the same DNA as an eighteen-year-old living in a yurt in Mongolia. But we aren't biological specimens. We're social creatures who live within the worlds of race, class, profession, gender, frat houses, faith communities, and so much more. Overcoming polarization requires the ability to see beyond our figured worlds by zooming out to problems we all care about. But this begins with understanding the figured worlds of which we're part and acknowledging our tendency to view people from other worlds suspiciously.

Opposites Don't Attract

Blondes prefer blondes. Brunettes prefer brunettes. Millennials would rather work with other millennials. And get this: An unusually high number of guys named Paul end up moving to Saint Paul, Minnesota. Far more Pauls live in Saint Paul than in any other US city.[3] Opposites don't attract. Research proves we're attracted to people like us. It's not so much that we consciously dislike people who are different from us, it's that we reserve our admiration, sympathy, and trust for people like ourselves, something described as "similarity attraction."[4]

Before you post a picture of you and your partner to prove me wrong, stop and reflect on this reality for a moment. There are certainly exceptions to similarity attraction. People marry across racial, political, and socioeconomic divides, not to mention falling in love with a partner with a different color of hair. But we're neurologically and socially wired to gravitate toward people like ourselves. In the workplace this is often described as "culture fit." Management says, "We decided to part ways because they just weren't a good fit." This is often code language for, "They're different." Our brains are predisposed to unconscious discrimination. In fact, trust decreases when we're exposed to people who speak and behave in unfamiliar ways.[5]

The fascinating thing about similarity attraction is how quickly we divide into us-versus-them groups, even when there's very little difference.

Turkish psychologist Muzafer Sherif examined this in his well-known social experiment called the Robbers Cave Experiment.[6] He and his colleagues brought two groups of twelve-year-old boys to camp. They were all white kids from similar middle-class backgrounds, and none of them knew each other prior to the study. Each group arrived at camp unaware of the other group. The first week, they bonded with their respective groups by hiking, swimming, sharing meals, and doing all the fun things you do at camp. They named themselves the Eagles and the Rattlers.

The second week of camp, the two groups were introduced to each other. Competitive activities were set up like baseball and tug-of-war, with the level of competition gradually increasing. Awards were given to the winning team. The competition escalated from name calling into burning each other's flags, vandalizing each other's property, and getting into physical fights. In a matter of hours, the boys did what we all do so easily—they created us-versus-them groups. Sherif and his team began to work on ways to break down the divisions. Fun activities were planned for the two groups to do together—shared meals, watching movies, and pairing boys from each group to swim, hike, or play ball. It didn't work. The boys still resorted to food fights, name calling, and brawling with the other side.

Dozens of other studies have found similar results. Researchers arbitrarily assign participants to different groups, sometimes with distinctions as meaningless as the "blue" group versus the "green" group, and sure enough, polarization rapidly emerges.[7] Just look how quickly a friendly sports competition or online discussion escalates into name calling and blocking people. If trivial differences polarize, it's little wonder that we vilify people who look and believe different than us. Many of our divides are double barreled, such as when your world of faith is combined with what you believe about gender and politics.

All too often, difference leads to violence. Anti-maskers shout at school principals and bully other parents for masking their kids. The same kind of vitriol comes from the other direction. In the midst of the Covid-19 pandemic, I saw someone post, "I don't care if unvaccinated people die, they deserve it." It's horrifying. There's enormous gravity to today's polarization.

Worlds Apart

One time I was sitting at a Starbucks in Kuala Lumpur. I noticed Umar, a young guy across from me, who looked like he might be a local, but based on his baseball cap, hoodie, earbuds, and backpack, he could have just as easily been from my Chicago neighborhood back home. He was multitasking between his phone, his computer, and talking briefly with people he recognized as they came and went. A while later, Umar and I ended up standing together outside at a taxi queue. We chatted and he asked: "So what are kids my age like in America?"

"Funny you should ask!" I said. "I was just thinking how much they look like you." We had a fascinating conversation about economics, politics, and religion. As we parted ways, Umar said, "Just remember, sir. I might look like the kids in your neighborhood on the outside. But what's on the inside is entirely different."

I used to say that two adolescents from opposite sides of the world have more in common with each other than either of them have with their own parents. And research backed me up. I surveyed youth from places as far apart as the United States, Brazil, Ghana, Taiwan, and Czech Republic. Teenagers across the world voiced a similar anxiety about the future, a desire to exert their independence, struggles with parents, and similar tastes in movies, fashion, and sports. In fact, a New York ad agency filmed teenagers' bedrooms in twenty-five countries around the globe. From the gear and posters on display in the teenagers' bedrooms, it was nearly impossible to tell whether the rooms were in Los Angeles, London, or Tokyo. In country after country, basketballs sat next to soccer balls; and closets overflowed with an international, unisex uniform of Levi's, Nikes, and baseball caps.[8]

Many adolescents across the planet share the world of youth culture. But when you look beyond the blue jeans and earbuds, you find that

Malaysian and US teenagers have starkly different views about life. Umar has been socialized to think about his education and career goals in light of what will be best for his parents, siblings, aunts, uncles, and grandparents. Simon has been told the world is his oyster and he should chase his dreams. These values have been instilled in Simon and Umar from an extremely early age. They undoubtedly share some similar interests and values as global youth, but those intersect with the values socialized in them from their figured worlds of place, race, and faith.

The figured worlds of family, school, friends, and work play a powerful role in shaping how we think and behave. One of my favorite examples is how the effects of drinking alcohol are as much a result of the social context as they are the body's reaction to the alcohol itself. One study found that students who believed they were drinking vodka and tonic at a bar began acting drunk within minutes of receiving what was actually only tonic water. The mere idea associated with drinking alcohol in a bar-like setting had a direct effect on their behavior.[9] People behave more refined and sophisticated when drinking French wine, and more gregarious and free-spirited when drinking Irish beer. The figured worlds associated with alcohol have a direct impact on behavior.[10] The same is true for Simon when drinking wine with his parents as compared to playing beer pong with his buddies. He will probably restrain exuberant behavior while sipping champagne at a family wedding, while letting loose and embracing his inner party animal when drinking the same amount of alcohol at a frat party.

What figured worlds hold the most significance for you? The places we grow up, the racial groups of which we're part, and the gendered scripts we've been handed have nothing to do with who we are as physical beings. Yet they have a profound impact on how we think and behave.

Shared Problems Unite

Our brains play a big part in how we interact with people from different figured worlds. Different regions of the brain are activated when someone from your in-group suffers as compared to someone from your out-group. This is one reason local and national news feature stories and disasters that affect people from our own communities more than those from the other side of the world. But our brains are malleable, and we can use that elasticity to focus on shared problems and overcome polarization.

One way our brains discriminate is that we give people like ourselves the benefit of the doubt, but we're unlikely to do so with people from different figured worlds. Using what psychologists call the fundamental attribution error, we excuse our team for breaking a rule because the other team was playing dirty. We conclude our team had no choice. But if the other team breaks a rule, we want the ref to call it immediately. If you're a Trump fan and he's accused of lying, fundamental attribution error makes you quick to give him a pass: "He didn't lie. He was just being humorous and sarcastic." But you're unlikely to allow for that nuance from a Democratic politician.

Stanford researcher Jennifer Eberhardt describes her experience as a young African American girl moving to a new, predominantly white high school in Ohio. "Every day," she says, "I was confronted with a mass of white faces that I could not distinguish from one another."[11] She met new peers, only to walk right by them the next day and wonder if they were the girls she'd had lunch with the day before. Eberhardt's admission is an example of what is called the "other race effect," or more often known by the cringeworthy statement, "They all look alike." Despite how bigoted that sounds, research shows that our brains are better at processing faces that evoke a sense of familiarity.

It's not that our brains are inherently biased. It's that our brains sort people into "friend" or "foe" based on what we "know" about people like them. If we're bombarded with messages that Muslims are terrorists or that Republicans hate immigrants, the regions of the brain that are associated with fear light up when we encounter those groups. When we see an out-group member we tagged as threatening, regardless of whether they really are, the region of the brain that processes fear is activated.[12]

The good news is the brain is not a hardwired machine. It's a malleable organ that responds to our environments and the challenges we face. When you reframe your orientation to focus on working with your polar opposite to solve a common problem, it can actually change your brain's neural wiring.[13] This is a critical insight for overcoming polarization, and it's something that was evident in the findings from Sherif's Robbers Cave Experiment. Shared problems are a proven way to overcome polarization.

It only took a matter of hours for the two groups of campers in Sherif's experiment to become enemies. Playing games together and spending time with each other did little to change the divisiveness. The researchers attempted to bridge the divides by creating obstacles that couldn't be solved unless the two groups worked together. The camp's water supply was shut off, and a truck bringing the campers food wouldn't start. At first, the groups only worked together long enough to resolve the specific challenge. But over time the continued pursuit of solving a common problem began to reduce the conflict. Name calling stopped, meals began to reflect intermingling between groups, and Eagle and Rattler friendships emerged. In addition, camp activities and leaders supported the Eagles and Rattlers working together. They provided direction and resources for working together to solve the various challenges. By the end of camp, the boys all rode the bus back home together, singing and laughing as one group.[14]

Sherif's experiment and hundreds of follow-up studies proved that working together to address shared problems is an essential part of overcoming polarization. It's absolutely critical for bridging our divided worlds, and it's a central theme informing the solutions throughout this book.

Transcend and Include

There's nothing wrong with being proud of the figured worlds of which we're part. Our in-groups provide us with meaning, connection, and security. The problem is when we dehumanize those from other figured worlds or become blind to the limitations of our own worlds. We all become actors in our figured worlds. We can accept the scripts of these worlds, improvise them, or leave them altogether. The worlds where we live don't get the final say on who we are. Our identity is always forming and reforming. Improvisation often occurs when we become part of other worlds that challenge the codes we previously learned, and we begin to rewrite our scripts. We transcend the figured worlds of which we're part while including parts of them in the new worlds we join.

Our differences don't have to polarize us. There are research-based strategies for transcending our divides by working together to solve shared problems. But first, we need to go one step deeper, because there's only one you and one me.

THREE

And Then There's You

How did a guy who grew up in a fundamentalist Baptist home in upstate New York end up globetrotting and writing books about cultural intelligence? I'm a Gen Xer, which means I was supposed to be a latch-key kid left to fend for myself while my parents pursued their careers. That's not my story, however. I'm the middle of three kids, and I had a stable upbringing, secure in my parents' love for God, each other, and me. Our family had a strong identity rooted in the figured worlds of which we were part, with faith at the center of it all.

My mom was the daughter of a successful Baptist preacher in Canada. My dad always wanted to be a minister, but somehow that never played out for him. But the church might as well have employed him. We were there all the time. On Sundays church was basically an all-day event with a brief break for lunch and my parents' afternoon naps. We were back at church at least two or three more nights every week. My parents were the bedrock of the church.

Like many people, I grew up with a very insulated view of the world. Our family's in-group revolved around people like us. We associated with people who looked like us, shared our religious beliefs, affirmed our political perspectives, and defined success and failure like we did. We were convinced our way was the one right way to view the world. In my early years there was very little room for people who sized up the world differently from me. "Different" equaled "wrong" or at the very least, "weird"! This wasn't just Christians versus other religions. It was our kind of Baptists versus everyone else. Even other so-called Christians were viewed with caution because their liberal views could lead down the slippery slope of relativism.

People often ask me how I ended up in this kind of work. I'm never quite sure how to respond. The easy answer is that my professional and academic pursuits led me across international borders, which inevitably brought me face-to-face with cultural differences. But cultural intelligence was not simply a professional pursuit. It became a way for me to hold together my increasingly complex, diverse worlds.

Seeing what all of humanity has in common and acknowledging the ways we're shaped by our figured worlds is an important part of becoming more culturally intelligent. But cultural intelligence ultimately requires an anthropological dig in our own souls. You and I can't be reduced to a list of cultural norms or human characteristics. We have agency to decide who we are and how we adapt to others. If I don't first know who I am, I can't hope to solve problems with others who come from entirely different worlds.

The 0.1 Percent Difference

Your DNA is 99.9 percent the same as everyone else's. But that remaining 0.1 percent translates into an infinite number of DNA pairings. More than one hundred billion people have walked the face of the earth, but no two people have ever been the same. There's only one you. And there's only one me.

I've taken a different path than my siblings. My brother is a pastor at a church three hours from where we grew up. Canada is the farthest he's traveled internationally. My little sister has lived within the same fifteen-minute radius her entire life and pretty much emulates the family traditions we had growing up as kids. Differences among siblings aren't unique to my family. I love hearing about the different paths pursued by kids growing up in the same home. We start in the same worlds of place, race, faith, and politics, but each of us charts our own path as adults.

Researchers have traditionally focused on the relationship between mother and child to understand family dynamics. But in more recent years the research has broadened to include other family relationships. Children aren't simply passive recipients in a family. My daughter Emily is a force. She assertively voices her opinions and is quick to take charge of what we should eat, how we should spend a holiday, and whether our values and beliefs are sound. My younger daughter Grace's spontaneous, adventurous spirit also shapes who we are as a family. She's the reason we vacationed in Ethiopia, and she talks us into watching some of the most bizarre TV shows. Some of my own beliefs and values have evolved based on my kids' thinking and experiences. I'm a reluctant dog owner because my kids talked us into it. I have a different perspective on women's modesty based on how my daughters and wife pushed me to think about it. Family values happen dynamically as the varied relationships are negotiated and influence each other.[1]

Growing up in my house, there was little room for nuance. Things were either right or wrong. Dancing, alcohol, rock music, sex outside of marriage—wrong! No exceptions. Going to church, evangelizing, tithing, reading your Bible—right! Baptists—right. Presbyterians—wrong. Other faiths weren't even a topic of discussion. Things were grayer when it came to political viewpoints, perhaps because my parents were Canadian and there wasn't the same level of alignment between evangelicalism and conservative politics. But most of life was viewed in black-and-white terms, a worldview I largely embraced.

My parents simply did what they thought was best and were largely following what their leaders told them they should do. And although there was an unusually strong religious orientation to my upbringing, a childhood with a strong worldview and a cohesive group is typical for most people. For the most part this is a healthy way to begin life and development. Psychologists argue that a healthy sense of identity begins with understanding and appreciating oneself before being able to appreciate the world and the reality of others. Protecting and caring for our own is not only okay, it's central to how the world works.[2]

As a Canadian family in the US, we occasionally talked about the cultural differences between the two countries, but beyond that my parents talked little about racial issues or our ethnicity. I can recall the occasional stereotypical comment about how Black people love nice cars or how interracial marriage is tough for kids, but that was about it. Race and family scholar Megan Underhill interviewed forty, white, middle-class parents in the US to examine how they talked with their kids about current events involving racial discrimination. The interviews were conducted following the shooting of African American Michael Brown Jr. in Ferguson, Missouri, by white police officer Darren Wilson. Even though the Ferguson protests were covered daily on the news and social media, most white parents had virtually no conversation about it with their kids. They believed doing so would bring unnecessary anxiety and stress, and in their minds, it didn't really affect their kids.[3]

In contrast, most African American parents talk about these issues with their kids all the time. Following the George Floyd murder in May 2020, many African American parents spent extensive time talking with their kids about the fear, stress, and anger that comes from wondering if one of their loved ones will be next. African American parents say they regularly talk with their kids about how to interact with law enforcement.[4]

Many of my African American colleagues and friends struggled to function at work in the days following the killings of George Floyd, Breonna Taylor, and Ahmaud Arbery. They found it disorienting to join virtual meetings with colleagues chatting about their weekend plans and favorite TV shows, as if there wasn't a care in the world. This is tricky because those of us not directly affected by these tragedies often aren't sure what to say. Many of us didn't grow up talking about these issues and are afraid of saying the wrong thing. But acknowledging the emotional toll that friends and colleagues may feel is a critical part of demonstrating support and care. Many people start life with an insulated view of the world through the figured world of their families. As we experience the broader world through school, media, and friends, however, we encounter other perspectives and values, some of which we may eventually embrace and make our own.

Outside Forces

One of the most important ways to understand identity development is to see the interaction between family contexts and the broader figured worlds of which we're part. Any basic textbook on sociology teaches that socialization begins in the home and is reinforced or challenged through school, media, peers, and eventually your professional life. For many of us, work is where we most encounter other figured worlds.

Maya is a project manager at a global company in Vancouver, British Columbia. Even though she doesn't travel for work, she works with contractors in India and Mexico every day. One of her biggest frustrations is managing deadlines and delays. She thinks that dismissing this as a cultural difference is just an excuse for incompetence and irresponsibility. For many Westerners like Maya, myself included, time is a prized commodity. *Time* is the most popular word in the English language.[5] Missing a deadline or consistently showing up late is seen as a profound sign of disrespect. But in other places around the world, schedules and deadlines seem arbitrary; any number of circumstances or priorities may supersede them. You grow up learning that an event begins when it begins. Life is not organized around arbitrary deadlines created before anyone knew what circumstances and unexpected events might occur.

Maya, however, believes most circumstances can be managed, and time is what you make it. Schedules and deadlines can almost always be met because the individual can control the outcome. One manager Maya works with in India is notorious for saying, "We're almost done," which Maya learned may mean next week, next month, or three months from now. Maya is responsible for seeing a project through, so it isn't very helpful when people tell her to relax and accept these cultural differences. She can't meet customers' expectations without timelines and consistent follow-through.

I talked with Maya about shifting her mind-set from managing the project to managing the relationship. Many individuals in places like India and Mexico approach tasks and trust-building within the context of relationship. The relationship needs to become the most important priority for Maya, something that is exceptionally difficult given that she's never met these individuals in real life. This might mean creating enough time on weekly calls to interact personally as well as to discuss the respective projects. Maya would benefit by co-developing the process with her overseas counterparts and regularly talking it through in light of their shared objectives rather than just managing the process through project management software. This approach might seem inefficient to some, but it's actually how projects most effectively get completed in most cultures.

Time is a value that's deeply ingrained in us from our families, schools, and society. Rather than trying to change someone's time orientation or simply tolerating the frustration, it's more effective to step back to understand what lies behind the differences and work to find a common problem. As Maya prioritized the relationship with her Indian and Mexican counterparts, they became more motivated to ensure that they didn't put her in a difficult position. This was far more valuable to them than simply meeting a deadline that felt unrealistic and arbitrary.

Intersecting Worlds

Kokei Saito is a thirty-two-year-old Brazilian who recently landed his dream job at an architectural firm in downtown São Paulo. The first time

I met Kokei, I couldn't entirely pinpoint his ethnicity. Everything about his warm, gregarious personality combined with his fast Portuguese exuded Brazilian. But there was something about his reserved demeanor that wasn't quite consistent with many of the young Brazilian professionals I know. Of course, with a population of more than two hundred million, what is a "typical Brazilian"?

Kokei, or Ko as his Brazilian friends call him, is a third-generation Japanese Brazilian. He loves a plate of *feijoada*, the traditional form of Brazilian rice and beans, just as much as he enjoys going out for sushi. He grew up in a relatively traditional Japanese home, where his parents instilled in him the three pillars of Japanese life—family, education, and work. Kokei started martial arts when he was four, and his parents primarily spoke Japanese at home. But Portuguese is his language of choice, and he has season tickets to Palmeiras games.

One of the challenges with many diversity seminars is the overemphasis on one aspect of our identities over others. I fall prey to this too. When I explain cultural intelligence, my default is to talk about differences in nationality—Germans versus Koreans, or Chileans versus Brazilians. Having spent so much time overseas, it's the easiest way for me to explain it. Some of my colleagues are more likely to explain CQ primarily through the lens of gender or race. But what aspect of Kokei's identity should his coworkers understand?

Kimberlé Crenshaw's groundbreaking work on intersectionality offers an essential perspective on how different parts of our identity intersect to shape who we are as individuals.[6] There's so much diversity within each of us. Let's assume you're being told how to work effectively with a Brazilian colleague. Which Brazilian do you mean? Do you mean a Brazilian born and raised in Toronto, someone who grew up in Rio but worked the past ten years in Silicon Valley, or someone like Kokei who grew up in a Japanese family in São Paulo? And how relevant is Kokei's identity as a queer, millennial, engineer?

None of us can be reduced to a single storyline. Our lives are multilayered. I'm a citizen of the US and Canada. I have a PhD. I'm white. I'm a dad. I'm a Christian. Any one of those labels carries with it all sorts of connotations. But only as we get to know each other can we really understand how we've each been shaped by the varied worlds of which we're part. No one storyline defines you or me. As we encounter the figured worlds of place, race, gender, faith, and politics, we discover it's impossible to talk about one of these worlds without another world also coming into view.

Which part of Kokei's cultural identity matters most to him? He's proud of his Japanese heritage. Having always been the minority in Brazil, being Japanese seemed like a more salient part of his identity, but when Kokei visited his extended family in Osaka, he suddenly felt like a complete foreigner. He discovered that his parents had adopted more of the Brazilian norms than he realized. While staying with his aunt and uncle in Osaka, Kokei was unnerved by the way his aunt waited on her husband and sons nonstop. Kokei's cousins seemed to be so much more reserved than his friends and family back home, and he found himself longing for a good *pao de queijo* to go with his morning coffee.

Crenshaw argues that movements like Feminism and Civil Rights can inadvertently ignore the complex issues facing marginalized groups.[7] People in an underrepresented group are often disadvantaged by multiple sources of oppression. Filipino women working in Dubai experience both racism and sexism, so campaigns to support them can't simply address one part of their identities. Their experiences are unique from Emirati women or Filipino men.

Take a moment to consider the figured worlds that shape you. What do you share with the figured worlds of which you're part? How do you deviate from them? Allow for the same kind of nuance as you relate to and work with others who are part of different worlds. Ask a friend from a different world to tell you something about life inside that world.

Like many young adults, I went through a period where I struggled with my identity. As a young, white, North American, Evangelical male,

I felt a growing angst that caused me to question what, if anything, I had to offer the world. The evangelistic proselytizing of my fundamentalist upbringing and the democracy building of my country conflicted with the ideals promoted in the sociology classes I was taking in grad school. I was compelled by the call to respect all people, whatever their beliefs and practices and to see the ills of globalization.

My wife and I were flying back to the US with our kids on 9/11. After the terror attacks that day, we were rerouted to Canada, where we had to stay for several days. By the time we finally landed in Chicago, my eyes welled up with tears as the airport personnel were there to greet us, waving American flags and celebrating our safe arrival to the homeland. It was the first time I felt patriotic in a long time. I began to see that commitment to my country didn't have to conflict with respecting and learning from other families, faiths, and nations. We were unified around addressing the problem of terrorism together.

It was also during this period that I began to find kindred spirits among associates and friends who didn't share my Christian faith. Some were Americans and many were from other parts of the world. It was both life-giving and disorienting to hear them argue for values and causes that I believed in, yet their reason for caring about problems such as polluted water, illiteracy, or war were rooted in a different religious tradition or none at all. My world was expanding. Not only did I sense a connection with Christians who were living around the world, I was developing a growing connection with people from other faiths and perspectives who were concerned about the same problems as me.

Lose the Labels?

A few years ago I gave a TechTalk on cultural intelligence at Google in London. As I fielded questions, one Irish woman prefaced her comments by saying that she had just completed two years working at Google's headquarters in California. She said, "I never thought about my coworkers as 'Americans.' I just interacted with them as individuals. I got to know Kate as Kate, Sanjay as Sanjay, and Jake as Jake." She argued that learning cultural norms puts people in boxes and instead we should just get to know people as individuals. One of the other Googlers spoke up and said, "I wonder how your experience would have been different if you had been in Cairo for two years instead of Silicon Valley. The very ways you got to know people may have been offensive from the start."

It's unrealistic and a bit disingenuous to say we simply interact with everyone as an individual without considering their cultural identities. We make split judgments about people as soon as we meet them. And we subconsciously put people in categories as soon as we get signals about their gender, ideology, and nationality. We need to move beyond those broad generalizations as quickly as possible, but we have to start somewhere. The wonder of who you are as an individual, juxtaposed with the 99.9 percent similarity you share with humanity everywhere, is the foundation for how we engage with our digital, diverse, and divided world. But how exactly do we get from that foundation to using our shared problems to overcome polarization?

PART II

Building a More Culturally Intelligent World

Identity politics, immigration reform, and protests are dividing families, communities, and workplaces. It's going to take more than joining a march or retweeting a statement to bridge the divide. We have to work together to solve problems that matter to all of us. Cultural intelligence (CQ®) gives us the tools to use our differences to come up with innovative solutions.

Cultural intelligence is the capability to relate and work with people who come from different figured worlds. While rooted in decades of peer-reviewed research, cultural intelligence is a practical model you can use to make sense of multicultural situations on-the-fly. Cultural intelligence doesn't require agreement. But it does mean opening ourselves up to consider *why* we think and believe what we do and how that shapes the way we relate to other people. It requires a unique mix of humility and self-confidence, and this is where cultural intelligence begins. Anyone can become more culturally intelligent. Let's begin with an up-close look at what cultural intelligence is, then we'll look at how to apply CQ personally and professionally.

FOUR

What's Your CQ?

Jared, a Foreign Service officer with the US State Department, asked me what a culturally intelligent response is when your beliefs and values conflict with those of another culture. His question wasn't theoretical. Jared is politically liberal and an ardent supporter of LGBTQ+ rights, but he spent several years working at the US embassy in Kampala, Uganda, where homosexuality is a criminal offense. The Trump administration issued an executive order against flying the LGBTQ+ flag at US embassies. But the first week in office, the Biden administration reversed it. Jared appreciated the bold move but immediately thought about the staff at the US embassy in Kampala, the majority of whom are Ugandan, not American. Not only do many Ugandans have personal beliefs against homosexuality, they live in a country where being homosexual can get you arrested or even killed.

What's a culturally intelligent way to respect Ugandans' beliefs and values while supporting the causes you believe in? On the one hand, diversity seminars and cross-cultural workshops laud the importance of respecting different worldviews and teach against imposing your values on others. Yet the US government and Jared are not neutral about LGBTQ+

rights. Like any of us who actively engage in today's diverse, digital world, Jared felt the dilemma of being inclusive and respectful while remaining true to his morals and convictions. Many of Jared's American colleagues were evangelistic in their attempts to convert Ugandan staff to accept LGBTQ+ as an acceptable way of life. They held mandatory training and confronted staff about their personal views. This didn't sit right with Jared, but neither did he feel comfortable simply looking the other way.

The dilemma of conflicting values and beliefs isn't unique to diplomats working overseas. This is territory we all have to navigate. When we work and relate with people from different backgrounds, even within the same community, the terrain keeps shifting. It's like driving somewhere and the GPS keeps rerouting. The complex, unpredictable nature of today's polarized world is what drove the development of cultural intelligence. My colleagues and I were interested in building on the large body of work studying cultural differences to understand what the twenty-first-century individual and organization can do to effectively bridge divided groups. The research started on the cusp of the new millennium; we never imagined what was awaiting us on the other side.

Genesis of CQ

From the very beginning, the research on cultural intelligence has been focused on going beyond cultural sensitivity to defining the *skills* needed to move in and out of many different worlds. How does someone like Jared retain his personal convictions while also engaging effectively and respectfully with Ugandan coworkers as well as the US and Ugandan governments? What does it look like to work on a project with a colleague who uses entirely different logic than you? The question that has continually driven our research on cultural intelligence is this: *What's the difference between individuals and organizations who succeed in today's diverse, globalized world and those that fail?* "Success" is defined as whether the individual or organization accomplished what they set out to do. Our purpose was not to evaluate whether individuals and organizations had the right objective, but instead, whether they had the skills to accomplish it in an unfamiliar context.

My friend and colleague Soon Ang, from Nanyang Technological University in Singapore, is one of the most fascinating people I know. Wicked smart and well-read on pretty much any topic, her voracious curiosity combined with her academic interests made her one of the pioneering researchers of cultural intelligence. In the late 1990s, Soon was consulting with a few multinational companies who were preparing for Y2K—the ticking time bomb that had everyone anxious about what would happen when the world's computers crossed from 1999 into 2000.

Soon was asked to help the companies' programmers work together to ensure readiness for December 31, 1999. She quickly observed that they were technically competent but struggling to collaborate. The brightest and most competent software engineers from around the world had been selected to work on this project. Yet despite weeklong meetings to agree on a global programming strategy, they went back to their respective locations and programed differently. The Germans did one thing, the Indians another, and the Filipinos something else. Before the next meeting, Soon recruited facilitators to run team-building activities. Modules were taught addressing soft skills like emotional intelligence and communication. There was a slight improvement in the implementation across regions but still too little alignment.

The clock was ticking toward December 31. This experience and others led Soon to conceive of a new capability that would eventually become known as CQ, short for "cultural intelligence quotient." She became convinced that adaptability and working effectively with people who have diverse backgrounds was no longer something only needed by diplomats, missionaries, or high-flying executives. It was a skill needed by everyone in the virtual, twenty-first-century workforce.

Meanwhile, I was in throes of researching the experiences of itinerant travelers. I was interested in how businesspeople, study-abroad students, and charitable volunteers engaged with the local cultures they encountered during relatively brief sojourns. Across multiple studies, I found individuals were ill prepared for the many unscripted conversations and situations they encountered. Travelers tended to focus on what they had in common with the locals or crass stereotypes. Many of the short-term missionaries I studied appeared oblivious to the message sent by showing up in a village sipping from a water bottle and lathering their hands with antibacterial solution. I continually observed culturally ignorant behavior from well-intended individuals who wanted to be respectful but were woefully missing the mark. But I wasn't content to be one more researcher critiquing "ugly Americans" without offering a solution.

A mutual colleague introduced me to Soon Ang and we immediately became friends. I was fascinated by her emerging work on CQ. As I studied her initial findings, I knew this was a research pursuit I wanted to join. The prospects were extremely bright for using CQ to help the kinds of individuals I felt called to serve. Today, the community of scholars studying cultural intelligence spans more than fifty countries with new findings published monthly. But the core emphasis has remained the same—how to effectively work and relate with people from any background amid a constantly changing, virtual world.

Four CQ Competencies

One of the consistent threads across varied forms of intelligence is a set of four complementary factors. These are found across emotional, social, practical, or cultural intelligence. The four factors are motivation, cognition, metacognition, and behavior.[1] A person who knows (cognition) how to relate interpersonally but has no desire to do so (motivation) won't function in a socially intelligent way. An individual who can analyze (metacognition) a practical situation deeply but can't actually solve it in real life (behavior) doesn't have much practical intelligence. In parallel fashion, cultural intelligence consists of four competencies—motivation (CQ Drive), cognition (CQ Knowledge), metacognition (CQ Strategy),

FIGURE 4.1 Cultural Intelligence competencies
By Grace Livermore, used with permission

and behavior (CQ Action). This is the academic foundation for all the practical solutions discussed throughout this book (Figure 4.1).

1. CQ Drive: Interest and Perseverance

CQ Drive is the level of interest, drive, and energy to deal with cultural differences. It's the degree to which you're open and interested to learn from different perspectives.

Travis is a second-generation Vietnamese American. He grew up in

Tennessee, went to college nearby, and got his first job out of college working for Young Life, a faith-based organization focused on adolescents. Travis became restless and convinced his fiancée to move to Palo Alto, California, to take a new assignment with Young Life. He describes the move to Palo Alto as the most difficult transition of his life. Everything felt alien—his neighbors, coworkers, even the churches. The pressing issues and topics of conversation felt foreign.

A few years later, Travis and his wife moved with Young Life again, this time to Singapore. That should have been the more disruptive move, particularly because it was at the very start of the Covid-19 pandemic. Yet Travis and his wife found the transition to Singapore much easier. Despite Travis's Vietnamese heritage, he's thoroughly American and has only been to Vietnam once. But his drive to understand the way of life in Singapore was much higher than his interest in Silicon Valley. It wasn't so much that he studied the culture more; it's that he had a different level of openness and curiosity that drove him to engage directly with the culture in Singapore as compared to Palo Alto. This is what it means to exercise CQ Drive.

CQ Drive is something any of us can develop. Four chapters into this book, you're well on your way. A great deal of what we covered in Part I can motivate us to do the hard work of bridging polarized worlds. CQ Drive begins by intentionally seeking interactions and experiences with people from different worlds with a goal of developing and maintaining relationships with people who see and experience the world differently than you. Working together to address problems we have in common is a key motivational driver.

Different ≠ weird. When my wife and I began traveling and living abroad with our kids, we repeatedly said to them, "Different, not weird." It's a mantra we've continued all throughout our family's travels. Eating noodles for breakfast isn't weird, it's different. Driving on the other side of the road isn't weird, it's different. Two straight men walking hand-in-hand isn't weird, it's different. It's a subtle but important way of framing how you view differences.

When you respond to another world's perspective with "That's weird!" stop and ask yourself, *Weird to whom?* Do the same thing when you hear yourself say, "That's just wrong." Many of the things we label as weird or wrong are simply unfamiliar to us. Cultural intelligence begins with an openness and interest in different ways of approaching life. Even moral dilemmas should start with a spirit of interest and curiosity before rushing to judgment. Being open to why Uganda believes homosexual behavior should be punishable by death is not condoning it. But we can't develop culturally intelligent solutions if we don't first take the time to genuinely understand the perspective behind it.

2. CQ Knowledge: Cultural Understanding

CQ Knowledge is your understanding of cultural differences and their role in shaping how people think and behave. This is the element most often emphasized when preparing to work cross-culturally. It's only one of the four competencies needed to bridge polarization but it's impossible to cross the divides if we don't first understand what's behind our differences.

Some people are confused why it's okay for a Black comedian to use the N-word and not a white person. The Black community rigorously debates whether there's ever an appropriate time to say it. A word is never just a word. It's rooted in context and this slur has a long history of symbolizing oppression and dehumanization. White slave masters, segregationists, and colonizers used the N-word to dehumanize Black individuals. So why would a Black person ever use it? Some say it's a way for the Black community to turn oppression on its head and use the term as a gesture of love and endearment, such as when comedian Larry Wilmore referred to President Obama as "my n*gga" at the White House Correspondents Dinner. Yet when white comedian Bill Maher used the word a few weeks later, he was forced to apologize. "It's like a knife, man," Ice Cube told him. "You can use it as a weapon, or you can use it as a tool....It's not cool because when I hear my homie say it, it don't feel like venom. When I hear a white person say it, it feel(s) like that knife stabbing you, even if they don't mean to."[2]

Doing the hard work to understand the historical and cultural significance of language is one way to build and apply CQ Knowledge. We never finish developing our CQ Knowledge. There's always more we can learn about different figured worlds. But an understanding of key similarities and differences between figured worlds is a good starting point, including things like communication norms, leadership preferences, risk tolerance, and time orientation. This broadened understanding gives us an ability to generate more accurate explanations for unfamiliar behaviors.

Seek to understand. This is another mantra I repeatedly use. Understanding why some groups are routinely punctual and others aren't begins with understanding. I don't have to agree with your behavior, but I must first understand what's behind it instead of writing you off as weird, ignorant, or brainwashed. This comes from talking to people from different backgrounds and by consulting evidence-based resources that provide knowledge about different figured worlds.

3. CQ Strategy: Awareness and Planning

CQ Strategy is the ability to "think about thinking." This competency enables a more nuanced approach to interacting with people from different figured worlds. Instead of simplistically teaching the dos and don'ts of Ugandan culture, the use of CQ Strategy considers things like the role of personal convictions, the cultural context, and the mission of the US government in Uganda.

Many assume that more information will solve problems. If we're struggling with a rebellious teenager, we look for a book to help. If people at work complain about millennials, we offer workshops about generational differences. Jared's colleagues assumed that educating Ugandan staff about the origins of sexual orientation would convert them to the cause. Books, training seminars, and graduate degrees are largely based on the premise that if we give people enough information, they will change their behavior. But that's just not true. We all have way more information than we need about eating healthy, exercising, saving for retirement, and flossing our teeth. But the challenge isn't lack of information. The same applies to many issues we face when reaching across divided worlds. In fact, mounting research shows that too much knowledge about cultural differences can actually be a handicap. Knowledge without the critical thinking and reflection that comes from CQ Strategy leads to overconfidence and real-world ignorance.[3]

CQ Strategy can be developed and applied by taking time to anticipate an intercultural interaction. This might be as simple as remembering to dress more formally when joining a business dinner in Paris than one in Silicon Valley, or it can mean having someone who understands Ugandan culture help you design a plan for how to appropriately raise a discussion about sexuality. CQ Strategy plays a critical role in overcoming polarization because it allows us to strategize how to address shared problems together.

Suspend judgment. Notice, don't respond. Check your assumptions. Suspend judgment. These are other mantras I often use, all of which link to CQ Strategy. When we fail to withhold judgment, we fall prey to generalizing an idiosyncratic behavior to an entire group. When observing an unfamiliar behavior, notice but don't immediately evaluate. CQ Strategy is the process used to plan, monitor, and assess our understanding and behavior—something that is incredibly difficult in the fast-paced, one-dimensional digital world. This helps us transfer what we learn from one world to another and eventually enables us to have a high degree of accuracy and consistency in anticipating and interpreting intercultural situations.

4. CQ Action: Flexibility

Finally, CQ Action is the ability to *act* appropriately in a wide range of intercultural situations. One of the most important priorities is knowing when to adapt and when *not* to adapt. Living in our increasingly diverse world requires the agency to tailor our responses to specific cultural contexts, while remaining true to ourselves.

Sylvia is a French executive working for a Middle Eastern company in Dubai. She's the only woman on the executive team, and the majority of leaders across the company are men. When interviewed for the position, Sylvia made it clear that she expected to be treated respectfully and equitably. They assured Sylvia they would respect her and demonstrated it with pay, title, and a direct reporting line to the CEO. Sylvia was unwilling to put on a submissive, deferential act to fit in with the male-dominated culture, but she found ways she could adapt to the cultural norms without losing herself in the process.

In France it wasn't uncommon for Sylvia to have lunch with a male colleague or client as a part of developing rapport and trust. But she avoids those kinds of lunches in her new role, believing it's one small way to respect the boundaries between work and personal interactions across genders. When Sylvia joins the executive team for a work-related dinner, she refrains from ordering alcohol. But when she discovered that the company was ignoring a number of safety regulations, putting their construction teams at risk, she raised the issue immediately. She communicated her concern respectfully but unapologetically and forcefully. This is what CQ Action looks like. Sylvia is comfortable in her own skin, and she's not trying to be all things to all people. But she adapts as needed to improve her effectiveness.

CQ Action comes with practice. It begins with trying different behaviors, like changing how quickly we speak, adjusting the way we greet people, or trying different ways to build rapport. Eventually we develop a broader repertoire of behaviors that we can use as needed. With time, we gain the ability to consistently adapt to differences while maintaining flexibility to ensure we don't overadapt.

Good intentions don't translate. During our first year of marriage, Linda and I were both in graduate school and working full-time jobs. There were few hours when our schedules overlapped. My idea of a good way to use the weekend was to get the house organized and cleaned for another week. Linda's idea was to do something fun together. I quickly learned that my good intentions didn't translate, another mantra I repeat when talking about cultural intelligence.

If someone experiences your behavior as sexist, your intentions don't matter. What matters is the impact of your behavior on the other person. Even during the time writing this book, I have been in situations when my behavior communicated something different than I intended. Whether it was attempting to use someone's mother tongue, poking fun at myself for mansplaining, or trying to navigate a tense conversation about racism, my communication didn't land quite right. I still feel defensive when called out on this kind of thing. *Do you know anything about me and my life work?!* But I'm getting better at putting aside my defensiveness, apologizing, and asking the other party if they would be willing to help me understand why my behavior was offensive and how I can be more respectful in the future. CQ Action means taking responsibility for adapting our behavior to ensure our intentions are expressed appropriately.

These four competencies give us the tools to navigate our digital, diverse, and divided world. But what does that look like in real life?

CQ in Real Life

Many people want dogmatic answers to complex issues. *If I'm having dinner with a Chinese person, should I offer to pay or not? Do millennials prefer working remotely or at the office? Should I text my African American friends after yet another innocent Black person has been shot?* The answer to all of these questions is "It depends!" What individual are you talking about? What's the nature of your relationship? Who has more power in this relationship? What's the goal?

But "It depends" isn't very helpful. What should we actually *do*? Do we just go with our gut and hope for the best? Please don't. The more differences there are, the more your gut is going to lead you astray. What might a culturally intelligent response look like when trying to figure out how to address LGBTQ+ issues in a place like Uganda? Or what do you do when a family member makes an outright racist comment?

The first step toward cultural intelligence is awareness of our own figured worlds. We learn that reacting based on our own norms and preferences might not be fair. Just because I prefer talking openly about a personal tragedy, doesn't mean you do. Or just because you think low taxes are the answer, doesn't mean it's the only right way. Self-awareness leads to an ability to recognize differences in other worlds and consider them as viable alternatives. The thing that really sets the culturally intelligent apart, however, is taking the time to proactively anticipate an intercultural situation so that you're better prepared. Mistakes are inevitable but the more you try, the more you'll become confident and adept navigating the unpredictability of people from so many different backgrounds.

Malena has been teaching third grade in Montreal for fifteen years. She's a favorite among parents and students so she was unsettled by how poorly her parent-teacher conference with a Burmese couple went. The family recently came to Canada as refugees, and Malena used her standard conference approach. She explained how their daughter was doing in class, shared a few samples of her work, and talked about some areas that needed improvement. But the parents just sat there and nodded, no matter what Malena said. Even when she asked them open-ended questions, they nodded or looked away. She thought it was a language barrier, but then she heard them talking freely with other parents in the hallway.

A teacher can't assume parents from different places have the same driving concerns and objectives for their kids, much less the same communication style. Academic achievement, critical thinking, and creativity have varying degrees of importance for people from different worlds. And Malena's teaching philosophy, which is focused on encouraging independent work, may seem inappropriate to parents from a collectivist place like Myanmar. Malena can't abandon the school's curriculum or teach differently for every student in her class, but we talked about how she could spend more time anticipating the driving concerns of the parents and developing ways to work together to address those needs through the school's curriculum. Malena met with them again, but this time she sent them an agenda ahead of time. She asked them to come prepared to discuss a couple specific topics, and she asked their sponsoring family to join them. This approach worked much better.

There's no one culturally intelligent way to approach any scenario. But culturally intelligent individuals focus on a common problem and use the four CQ competencies to work together to solve it.

An American who supports LGBTQ+ rights may be tempted to pressure Ugandan staff to adopt the US position, or they might ignore the Ugandans' perspective altogether. Many of the Americans working at the embassy organized several training sessions for the Ugandan staff to educate them about the origins of sexual orientation and the importance of LGBTQ+ rights for any democratic society. Some of them asked the Ugandan staff for a compromise: "You don't have to personally agree with this view, but you need to support this as a part of your job." This is more effective than ignoring their perspective altogether, but Jared and I discussed a different way of applying CQ to this situation.

Respect and dignity are core values of Ugandan culture. The Ugandan government and citizens want to create a better way of life for everyone. So addressing dissenting views on LGBTQ+ rights requires more than raising a flag and holding a couple of seminars on sexual orientation. Jared needs to zoom wide enough to find a common problem. At the time of writing, the Ugandan government is advancing legislation to prevent sexual harassment and assault. Jared may not convince Ugandan leaders that homosexuality is an acceptable lifestyle, but he may more easily get them to agree that all Ugandans, regardless of their sexual orientation, should be protected from assault. In addition, he can find allies in people like Rita, a Ugandan mother who is religiously opposed to homosexuality but doesn't want her gay son imprisoned for it. These kinds of incremental steps are rooted in the shared concern for protecting all Ugandans and drawing on Ugandans' core belief that all its citizens are God's children. This process is slow but more likely to lead to lasting change together.

GPS for a Moving Destination

Whether you're an overseas diplomat or a project manager working remotely from home, we're all working with people who have vastly different backgrounds. You need cultural intelligence to build trust with team members you've never met in real life. You need it to figure out ways to address conflict with people from different worlds. And you need CQ to reconcile your own convictions and values with those of other individuals, organizations, and cultures. It starts with zooming out to a common problem and using cultural intelligence to address it.

Cultural intelligence isn't innate. It's a skill any of us can develop to improve the way we navigate our digital, diverse world. Dozens of peer-reviewed studies demonstrate that CQ is malleable.[4] Direct experience, education, accountability, and reflection are all tools for improving CQ. But what's a culturally intelligent way to talk to your racist uncle or sexist coworker?

FIVE

How to Navigate Polarizing Conversations

You board a flight, and a female captain with a thick southern accent welcomes everyone. Your seatmate mumbles, "Well that doesn't make me feel safe."

A high-school classmate posts a joke on social media. "Stuck on a math problem. Any smart Asians want to help me?"

Your uncle says, "I don't have a racist bone in my body, but I'm sick of certain groups crying about the past all the time. Learn how to work hard work and you'll be fine."

These aren't people heading off to a white supremacist rally. They're our friends, family, and neighbors. They're quick to condemn homophobia, racism, or sexism, yet they frequently make cringeworthy statements laced with bias and prejudice. When should you confront bias? How do you do it? And when do you need to take a deep breath, choose your battles, and move on? Almost any time I give a talk on cultural intelligence, people ask, "How do we get the people who *aren't* here to care about this?" What about all the people who think diversity is overplayed? They're quick to condemn overt bigotry, and they have friends and family from different backgrounds. But they believe too much is being made of issues like race, privilege, and sexuality.

This is a chapter about how to apply cultural intelligence to polarizing conversations. If you're part of a marginalized group, you might decide to opt out of these conversations given the emotional toll involved. You have my complete respect and support. But if you're reading this book, I'm guessing you may be looking for ways to engage in conversations with friends and loved ones who don't get it. Before we dive into this complicated topic, I want to say a couple things up front.

First, while this chapter is about navigating polarizing conversations, I've decided to show how to do it when confronting racism since it's one of the most volatile topics in our digital, diverse world. But these conversational strategies apply whether we're discussing racism, sexism, homophobia, ideological zealotry, or other forms of bigotry. Second, I'm sometimes racist and you might be too. Not all the time; I'm far less likely to engage in racist thinking and behavior today than I did thirty years ago. But I've never met someone making progress on this journey who says, "I'm not racist." So let's beware that we're all susceptible to racism and other forms of bias and discrimination. Here are some culturally intelligent ways to navigate these conversations.*

Be Clear about Your Goal

Having a conversation about polarizing issues like racism begins with CQ Drive, the motivational component of cultural intelligence. CQ Drive gives us the needed energy and confidence. We have to identify what we hope to accomplish when confronting racist thinking and behavior. Exposing someone to their racist attitudes doesn't produce results quickly, and it's unlikely you'll get there with a snap condemnation

*Each of these solutions begins with one of the four CQ competencies (e.g., CQ Drive), but other CQ competencies are also part of each solution. For example, being clear about the goal is linked to CQ Drive because it provides the motivation for bridging the differences; but clarity about the goal also requires understanding (CQ Knowledge) and awareness (CQ Strategy).

"You're so racist." Calling someone a racist never results in someone saying, "Oh, wow. You're right!"

Given the effort and perseverance required to effectively confront racism, we need to focus on a few individuals with whom we can make the commitment. If I overhear an offensive comment by a stranger in the supermarket, I don't have the option of taking a long-term approach. Perhaps all I can do is speak up and challenge their thinking. But I'm primarily interested in how we apply cultural intelligence to the people who are a regular part of our lives.

Steve and Eric grew up in a Seattle suburb. During high school they were inseparable. They played soccer together, worked together at the local YMCA, and even vacationed with each other's families. While their high school was predominantly white, they had a couple teammates who weren't. Steve left the Pacific Northwest to attend Washington University in Saint Louis, Missouri. Eric stayed home and attended community college for a couple years before working full-time for his uncle's construction company. Steve and Eric get together when Steve comes home to visit, but that is becoming less frequent, particularly since Steve graduated from college and started a full-time job in Chicago.

Recently, Steve has been unnerved by Eric's posts on social media in response to racial protests occurring in Seattle. Eric was never very engaged in current events, but he has suddenly become very outspoken with social media posts like: "People need to respect authority." "Quit bitching about the past and get a job." And the post that pushed Steve over the edge: "All Lives Matter. Enough said." Steve hadn't engaged with any of Eric's posts, but he replied to the "All Lives Matter" post by responding, "Exactly! Which is why it's so appalling that Black lives seem so dispensable in this country." Eric responded: "Sorry, bro. Not drinking the woke Kool-Aid like you are."

These kinds of situations get heated fast. If we're going to have a constructive conversation, we need to first go beneath the surface to understand what's driving the conflict. People rarely think of themselves as consciously dehumanizing someone because of the color of their skin. It usually rests in some deeply rooted fears and uncertainties.

It's also important to pay attention to our own mental state when deciding how to confront racism. I saw a friend posting racist vitriol on social media at a time when I was dealing with a massive business challenge. I had zero headspace to think about how to confront her, but I couldn't remain silent. I fired off a terse comment that was public. While my comment received a lot of "likes," it only riled up my friend further. I later messaged her privately and we eventually talked. But in retrospect it would have been better if I had held off responding and had instead contacted her when I wasn't in the middle of a crisis. We all have to weigh the energy and drive required to do this work, with the onus of responsibility on dominant racial groups.

Understand Their Point of View

Next, we need to use CQ Knowledge to understand the values and norms that guide the other individual's thinking and behavior. Think about this like you do when trying to understand someone from a different part of the world. What are the beliefs, values, and assumptions underlying their behavior? Many may not be able to tell you. Someone who thinks it's ridiculous to change the name "Blackhawks" for a sports team, might not be able to articulate their reasoning.

Taking time to understand someone's racist perspective is uncomfortable. We're not talking about benign differences like understanding why you hate coffee and why I love it. This is about confronting bigotry. But if we're going to truly engage in dialogue, we need to acknowledge that there are almost always concerns and perspectives that have more to do with the individual's own life than with the systems of oppression in which they operate. Many white working-class individuals feel like affirmative action programs put them at a disadvantage. Conservative faculty believe they have a harder time earning tenure than their liberal peers. It's critical to actively understand the perspective that lies beneath the biased perspectives we want to confront.

One of the most important ways to address polarization is through perspective-taking—the capability to step outside our own experiences to imagine the emotions, perceptions, and motivations of another individual.[1] Most of us engage in perspective-taking all the time. *What would my daughter like for her birthday? Where would my friend like to eat dinner? How will I convince this prospect to close the deal?* There are multiple ways to use perspective-taking when confronting racism.

Adam Galinsky, one of the foremost researchers on perspective-taking, led a study where students were shown a photo of an elderly man sitting on a chair next to a newspaper stand. The students were asked to write a short essay about a typical day for this man. One-third of the students were given no further instructions. They were told to simply look at the picture and describe the man's day. This was the control group. The next third was simply cautioned against using stereotypes to describe the man's day. The final third was directed to write the essay in the first-person, as if they were the man in the picture.

Many of the students in the control group used a lot of negative stereotypes to describe the man, including his loneliness, his dependency on others, and his declining physical and mental health. The students who were told to avoid stereotypical language wrote more neutral descriptions about the man's day, making up scenarios about how he might spend his time and what he thinks about. But the students who were asked to write the essay in first-person perspective wrote the most positive descriptions of this man's life, with references to his sage wisdom, his wide range of friendships, and the joy he finds in the simple things of life. Perspective-taking increases the likelihood that individuals will not only be less discriminatory in their thoughts and behaviors but will actually develop more positive viewpoints.[2]

As Steve thought about how to engage with Eric, he didn't write a "day in the life of Eric" essay, but he did commit to watching a half hour of Fox News every night for a week. In some ways it made him feel even more daunted about talking to Eric. But it also gave him better insight into Eric's perspective. Hosts like Sean Hannity, Tucker Carlson, and Laura

Ingraham consistently referred to the "Black Lives Matter mob," and almost nightly there was a segment that featured the grievances of white America. Features and commentaries focused on immigrant crimes and the "real" story behind the questionable behavior of a Black man killed by a police officer. Steve was a strong believer in the realities of systemic racism and implicit bias, and it riled him up to hear this propaganda. But consuming Fox News for a week helped him better understand where Eric was coming from. Steve thought some of the content was sheer nonsense, but there were also legitimate concerns coming through.

Steve was particularly struck by an interview with an economist who was talking about the gutting of manufacturing jobs across the US for the past thirty years. The economist said that working-class families like Eric's have had the lowest upward mobility rates in the US for the past several decades. For many years manufacturing and construction provided a decent living so that people without college degrees could easily live a stable, middle-class life. But that's not the case anymore. For average workers in the US, wages haven't increased beyond inflation for thirty years, while incomes for high-wage positions have soared.[3] Of course, being poor and Black is a double strike against the chances of upward mobility, something that wasn't mentioned in the news segment. But working-class whites are too often pitted against working-class people of color, rather than seeing the shared needs of both groups.

Taking the time to listen to the other side prepares us for a more constructive dialogue. Watching to Fox News provided Steve with a better understanding of what may be behind Eric's frustration with so-called identity politics.

Map the Conversation

The next step is to use CQ Strategy to map a conversation with a friend who seems blind to racism. This might mean jotting down a few notes or talking through your plan with another friend beforehand. Run through

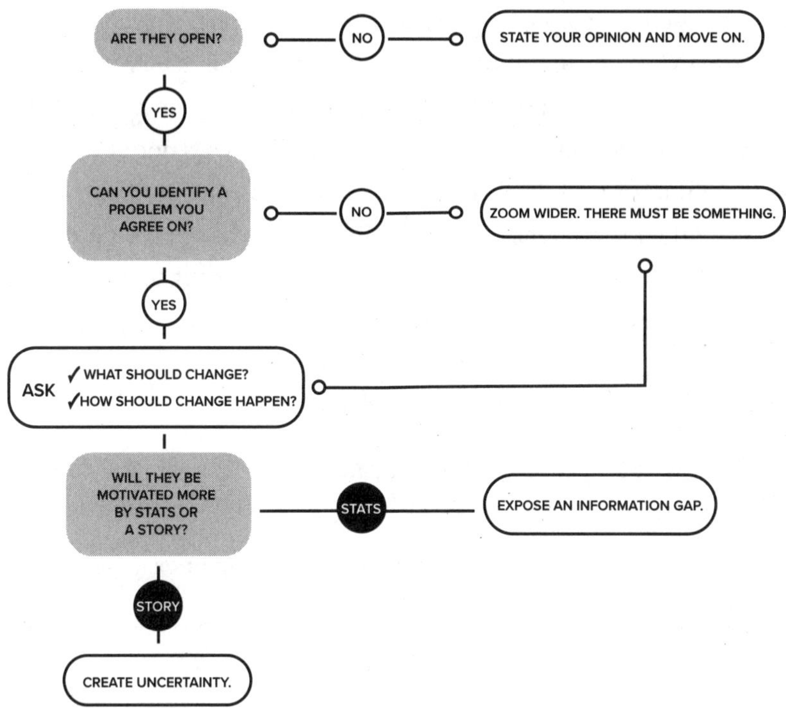

FIGURE 5.1 How to discuss polarizing issues
By Grace Livermore, used with permission

some "if-then" scenarios to anticipate how you will respond if they make a certain statement. Anticipate the time and place that will be most conducive to this kind of dialogue (e.g., probably not on social media or at a large family gathering). The research on cultural intelligence offers some specific strategies to prepare for these critical conversations (Figure 5.1).

Open or Closed?

Anyone can become more culturally intelligent and less racist. But you can never force someone to improve their CQ Drive and care about these issues. You have to evaluate whether they're open to rethinking their assumptions. Research repeatedly shows that preaching at people who are closed to your perspective does little good and, worse yet, it can lead them to become more entrenched, emboldened, and dogmatic about what they believe. Studies show that arguing with dogmatic individuals who are vehemently closed to alternative perspectives is not only pointless, it's counterproductive.[4] An individual who is convinced that Black people are their own worst enemies is unlikely to change their attitudes and beliefs just because you present a logical argument to show them how wrong they are. When a closed person is told they're misinformed, it results in the individual being even more certain and confident in their own perspective than they were in the first place.[5]

+ They ask open-ended questions, demonstrating a genuine desire to understand.
+ They're willing to admit a statement was wrong or exaggerated.
+ They can point to something they respect about the "other" side, and something that troubles them about "their" side.
+ They aren't afraid to say, "I don't know."

If you encounter a friend or family member who is closed, state your view and move on. If they show even the slightest openness, move forward by using what the counseling field calls motivational interviewing.

What Should Change?

Motivational interviewing taps the individual's own drivers rather than trying to force change. Something is motivating Eric to suddenly engage in the conversation on race. Instead of telling him how racist he is, it's far more effective to explore what Eric wants to see change. Does he really think discrimination against Black individuals is nonexistent? Or does he feel like people like him are presumed to have a silver spoon in his mouth, just because he's white?

If Eric is open, Steve might try questions like:

+ You never say anything controversial on social media, but you've suddenly been very vocal about this. What is it about this that really gets under your skin?
+ What do you think people (e.g., the media) get wrong about how you feel?
+ How would you like things to be different?

Resist the urge to challenge the responses. This is going to be hard, especially if Eric spouts off propaganda from faulty sources. But the purpose is to listen and help him articulate his thoughts and attitudes. If Eric is open to the possibility that there might be more than occasional incidents of discrimination, you have an opportunity to build from that. There's extensive research supporting the effectiveness of motivational interviewing to elicit behavior change. It's used as a catalyst to help individuals overcome drug addiction, eating disorders, and gambling, and it's used to reconcile estranged family members. Large-scale studies have shown that motivational interviewing far outperforms advice-giving when seeking to provoke a change in behavior and thinking.[6]

How Should Change Happen?

Pay attention to *how* your friend wants to see change happen. Push them to explain the "how" rather than just repeating the "what." *How would you address inequitable pay, disproportionate rates of arrest, health disparities, etc.? How would you promote better opportunities for all working-class people, regardless of race?*

A study on political extremism found that many citizens had very little understanding of the policies they opposed or supported. They just knew that something didn't sit right with them. But individuals were more willing to open their minds to alternative approaches when they were asked *how* their preferred policies would work. Having to talk through the complexities of health-care legislation or immigration policy caused the individuals to see the nuance of the situation and acknowledge gaps in their knowledge.[7]

Organizational psychologist Adam Grant used motivational interviewing when talking with an antivaxxer friend who said that vaccines can't be relied on to stop a pandemic. Prevention and treatment should be prioritized. Grant asked him whether vaccines could be part of the strategy, and his friend replied, "Yes. For some people." Adam saw that as an opening. He asked his friend what the odds were that he would get a Covid vaccine. His friend said it was unlikely but not out of the question. "This is not a black-and-white issue," he told Adam. "My views change."[8] That kind of statement indicates an openness to nuance, and it might be fodder for finding common ground. Once you agree on the problem, you can begin to move toward solutions.

Stats or Stories?

Next, gather data to support your conversation. Some people are moved by compelling stories and others by statistics. Use what you know about your friend to prepare evidence that will most likely catalyze them to think deeper. Research demonstrates that the two most powerful ways to pique curiosity are exposing an information gap and uncertainty.[9] This might mean asking questions like:

+ How do you explain that 25 percent of Black job candidates received callbacks when they "whitened" their résumés but only 10 percent did when they left in details indicating they were Black (e.g., name, affiliations, awards, etc.).
+ Have you ever had a friend or colleague who was treated differently because of the color of their skin?

Have a couple data points ready to pique your friend's curiosity, not as ammunition but to catalyze discussion and align around a common problem. And be willing to consider counterpoint data from your friend.

Culturally Intelligent Dialogue

Finally, it's time to talk, which requires CQ Action so that you avoid language and behavior that needlessly polarizes. Ideally, use your CQ Strategy in advance to consider everything I've laid out before sitting down with your friend. Varying degrees of assertiveness are necessary to confront racism with our friends and family. The goal is to retain the relationship while addressing the injustice. It might be useful to establish some rules of engagement like the following:

Argue Like You're Right. Listen Like You're Wrong.

This is one of my favorite Adam Grant quotes. Beginning with a resolve to speak with confidence and listen with humility gives us the passion and discipline needed for a productive conversation.

Steve and Eric decided to FaceTime because it had been a while since they had communicated beyond texts and messages. Soon into their conversation, Eric made the classic rebuttal, "Don't blame me. I never owned slaves." Steve said, "Okay—you're right. Me either. So, tell me why it's so offensive to be asked to acknowledge something for which neither of us have any direct responsibility." There were many times when Steve wanted to challenge Eric, and more than once Steve rolled his eyes and said, "Oh my god. What are you even talking about?" Steve told Eric that he agrees neither of them should be blamed for slavery just because they're white; but he thinks it's important to acknowledge the lasting impact slavery has had on Black people in the US as well as the long-term privileges it's given white people.

See if you can explain each other's perspective without debunking it or criticizing it. This may mean Steve says something to Eric like, "You think it's completely unfair that you're asked to take responsibility for something that happened long before you were alive. And it's offensive to you when people call you 'privileged' given the sacrifices and hard work you've put into making a life for yourself." Allow your friend to correct you if you misrepresent their perspective. If you don't accurately understand each other's perspective, it's impossible to have a meaningful dialogue.

Practice First-Person Perspective-Taking

Next, Steve needs to find a way for Eric to personalize a Black person's perspective. It's a lot harder to make dogmatic, sweeping statements about entire out-groups when you personalize their story. See if your friend can imagine what their life would be like if everything was the same except for their race. Here's where the data you gathered ahead of time can help. You can prompt the conversation with a fact or an anecdote. Eric and Steve might imagine what their experience on the soccer field may have been like if they had been Black or Asian. Eric might consider what homeowners might say or think if he showed up at a jobsite as a Black guy with dreadlocks.

Eric was particularly worked up over the needs of white working-class people. Steve would also benefit by personalizing what it would be like if he hadn't gone away to college and instead had heard local politicians continually talking about racism and privilege with zero attention given to the devastation of factory towns emptied out by the tech boom.

Heat It Up or Cool It Down?

Keep your hand on the temperature of the conversation. This is one of the trickiest things to navigate. For dialogue about racism to be constructive, there needs to be enough discomfort to foster productive reflection and change but not so much that our friends shut down and become defensive. If the temperature becomes too cold and theoretical, people won't feel the need to ask uncomfortable questions or make difficult decisions. If it gets too hot, people will dismiss it altogether or simply become more calcified in what they already thought.

Regulating the temperature of a conversation includes monitoring our friends' current state. My daughter Grace was in a serious cycling accident in a national forest in Ireland. It took an emergency rescue team five hours to get her to the hospital, followed by a lengthy surgery. The same day of her accident, another girl her age fell in the same forest, broke her back, and was told she would never walk again. When Grace was lying in agony, I didn't say, "Well, at least you're not paralyzed." Minimizing someone's pain and struggle by telling them someone else has it worse is not only ineffective; it lacks compassion and empathy.

Screaming "you're privileged" to someone who grew up in a trailer park with a single parent is tone-deaf. Only in very specific circumstances would any reasonable person ask a white person in abject poverty to consider their white privilege. Grace herself later reflected on how fortunate she is that her accident was not worse. But to build awareness and foster perspective-taking, we should always avoid dismissing the reality of someone's struggle and unique story.

Take the Long View

Eric didn't confess to being a racist. But he conceded that their friends of color face some unfair realities. There isn't a clear path for discussing these issues. Part of being culturally intelligent is becoming comfortable with the absence of simplicity and clear solutions while continuing to do the hard work. But these conversational strategies provide a GPS for navigating this unpredictable terrain.

I've watched countless people reconsider their perspectives and move one step forward in the journey toward building a more culturally intelligent world by applying these conversational tools. Don't try to change people's minds; you can't. But if you can help them understand their thinking, it can open them up to rethinking. The rest is up to them.[10]

SIX

How to Compete with Robots

Listen to many futurists and you would think that robotic engineers and therapists will be the only people with jobs in ten years. There's plenty of reason to pay attention to the massive disruption from the automation of work. But if you've ever attempted to do a virtual chat session with a customer service robot or been frustrated talking to a voice-activated receptionist, you know there's plenty of work left for humans.

CNN medical correspondent and neurosurgeon Sanjay Gupta says, "No matter how sophisticated artificial intelligence becomes, there will always be some things the human brain can do that no computer can."[1] But having a brain isn't enough. It's using the power of this small, mighty organ to do what technology can't do nearly as well—adapt and create. Joseph Aoun, president of Northeastern University, says students need to be prepared to work alongside smart machines. Rather than taking a dystopian view of a world overrun by robots, Aoun argues that humans should focus on what we alone can do: exercise our cognitive abilities to invest, discover, and create something valuable to society. And in his view this comes down to developing human literacy—flexible thinking, creativity, and cultural agility. In other words, cultural intelligence.[2]

Our jobs, more than anywhere else, are where we're most likely to interact with people who have vastly different beliefs and values. I don't have the option of ignoring colleagues who disagree with me about sexuality, climate change, or racial injustice. I'm expected to join meetings, exchange emails, and send messages to people who come from vastly different figured worlds. Although robots beat humans in cognitive competitions like chess and complicated math problems, they lack the human agility, compassion, and understanding to address the polarizing issues that impede workplace effectiveness. But if we aren't careful, we as humans can also behave robotically. Cultural intelligence leverages our human skills to work with colleagues from vastly different backgrounds to come up with innovative solutions that have a direct impact on organizational effectiveness.

Reading People

One of the most important skills needed in today's workplace is an ability to read people. Managers' ability to assess engagement, graphic designers' grasp of clients' wishes, and mechanics' conversations with customers are all affected by how accurately they read people. Without CQ, you lack the ability to read people's cues any better than robots, particularly people from different backgrounds.

Many hospitals have safety policies where medical staff are instructed to record any indication that a patient or family member may be violent. The hospitals have a coding system where staff put a red "V" on a patient's chart when they observe potentially violent behavior. One US hospital administrator told me he sees a troubling pattern. Most of the patients labeled "violent" come from different cultural backgrounds than the dominant culture in his local community. He said, "Midwest etiquette says you express disappointment and anxiety in calm, measured ways. Tears are understandable but losing your cool isn't." Many of the patients labeled "violent" were described as yelling, crying uncontrollably, and in some cases wailing. Are these people violent, or do they just have a different way of expressing emotion? Reading people is enormously more difficult when the cultural cues change.

A psychologist with one of the largest police departments in the US described a similar situation. His chief responsibility is focused on assessing and mitigating threats across Los Angeles County, a diverse metropolitan area of over ten million people. "Seventy-five percent of what we deal with requires high levels of cultural intelligence," he said. "Our officers have not been trained to know whether someone from a different cultural background is exhibiting a behavior that should be considered a potential threat, mental illness, a culturally derived emotional response to crisis, or some combination thereof."[3] To make matters worse, law enforcement is increasingly expected to evaluate people through their online behavior.

Robots are woefully inept at reading people. But it's not easy for humans either, especially during virtual interactions. With cultural intelligence, however, we can pick up on cues to understand what lies beneath behavior. A great deal of what these medical professionals and law enforcement officers encounter is a difference described as neutral versus affective behavior. Neutral-oriented cultures believe that minimizing emotional expressiveness is a sign of dignity and respect, whereas an affective orientation values expressing feelings.[4]

The Canadian home where I grew up was characterized by neutral communication. We used formal manners at the dinner table, fine china was on the table for Sunday dinner, and you *never* interrupted anyone. This rule guided our family protocol, and it informed the way we evaluated other people's behavior. To this day, I become uncomfortable when someone interrupts because that was such a taboo in my family. In neutral-oriented cultures, interruptions are considered rude unless an emergency calls for it. Whereas in affective-oriented worlds, interruptions are okay and may even show how interested you are in the conversation. In many neutral-oriented cultures, particularly throughout many parts of Asia, silence is not only okay, it's welcomed. Silence is considered a sign of respect, and it allows both parties to reflect and take in what has been said. In many affective-oriented cultures, however, silence is viewed as punitive. Move these conversations to Zoom and it becomes all the more complicated.

Nurses and police officers may wrongfully label someone as violent because of an affective response and may overlook violence from a neutral-oriented communicator. There are terrorists who never scream and shout. And there are people who scream and shout who aren't violent. Managers may assume a neutral-oriented staff member is disengaged, when in fact they may have a different way of expressing their enthusiasm. And team members may assume a teammate has a temper, when in fact they may simply have a different value for how openly and passionately to voice their opinions.

Or what about the different norms around direct versus indirect communication? Many of us have learned that the most respectful way to address conflict is to respect someone enough to talk to them about it directly. Yet others have learned that respect means acknowledging we're both intelligent enough to know that there's a conflict going on without needing to lose face by explicitly discussing it. These are just a couple of examples of how challenging and important it is to develop the human skill to read people who have been socialized differently than you. It's the kind of skill that Qatar Airways has prioritized in training their cabin crew. They recognize that luxury equipment and entertainment systems don't set them apart from Emirates or Singapore Airlines. Instead, it's the ability to provide five-star service with crew who accurately read customers from many different worlds and serve them with a personalized touch that stands apart from the robotic approach that's become all too familiar in many businesses.

One of the best ways to get better at reading people is to become familiar with a few key values that distinguish one figured world from another. These include communication differences like the ones I just mentioned—neutral versus affective and direct versus indirect communication; but there are several other cultural value dimensions that can help us read differences, including leadership preferences, work habits, risk-tolerance, and motivational drivers. Look for whether someone indicates a preference for working autonomously, reflecting a more individualist orientation, or working with a group, a more collectivist orientation. Another value difference that often creates conflict on work teams is varying levels of comfort with ambiguity and uncertainty, something strongly shaped by the worlds of which we're part. To what degree does a direct-report value detailed plans and procedures? Or do they prefer that you let them figure things out on their own and learn by trial and error? Far too often, differences in these values are wrongfully used to categorize someone as incompetent, when in fact, it may simply reflect different ways of approaching one's work.

In the global digital age, it's not overly useful to memorize which cultural groups have which value preferences, because unlike robots, we don't always act as we're programmed. A colleague's behavior, particularly in the work environment, may be more strongly shaped by the organizational culture or their role than by their national, ethnic, or gender identity. But look for cues that indicate their value preferences. You can find more information about these cultural values online and through other books that address them more fully.[5]

Presenting Yourself

Another critical way to stand apart from robots is to manage how you present yourself to others. First impressions emerge within seven seconds of meeting. One study found that we only have a millisecond before people size up whether we're trustworthy.[6] People read you just as much as you read them. Robots don't care what people think about them or the context they're in. They behave consistent with how they're programmed to behave. But culturally intelligent humans read a situation and present themselves accordingly. International students tell me that the most intimidating part of interviewing for jobs is the unscripted portion. *What do you say when you're sitting at the table and waiting for the interview to get started? What about when the person hosting you walks you to the elevator or has lunch with you?* They're right to be concerned. A job candidate's likability and trustworthiness may be judged far more based on how they behave informally than during the formal interview. It's not fair. Robots aren't judged for their likability and trustworthiness, but we are.

When I give a keynote presentation, I often begin with a brief personal story. For me, it's a more interesting way to introduce myself than using a scripted, robotic bio. One time I was speaking in China and my interpreter didn't translate my opening anecdote. She said something like "Our speaker is doing what a lot of North American speakers do. He's telling a story he thinks is funny." I continued, assuming she was sharing a story that had consistently worked so well for me elsewhere. She assured the audience she would translate as soon as the story was done. She even asked the audience to laugh on cue so I wouldn't feel bad. Sure enough, just as I got to the funny part of the story, the crowd erupted with laughter. I read this as, *Wow! This is going great. Even my humor is translating well.* Only later did someone fill me in on what happened.

There are articles all across the web that tell you what behaviors create a good first impression professionally, including how to dress, your handshake, and your ability to make small talk. But far too much of this advice assumes a robotic approach that doesn't account for the situation.

What was it about my introductory story in China that didn't work? It turns out that my translator and the organizers who brought me to China felt that starting with a self-effacing story was embarrassing to them and the audience. People came expecting to hear from an expert, but to them, my opening illustration presented me as someone who didn't know what he was talking about. First impressions count, especially at work. A robot could have easily read a transcript of my presentation in flawless Mandarin. But that's not what we want from a speaker. We want to hear from someone who is authentic and real, which raises the question: When should we adapt, and when is adapting compromising our authenticity?

One time I led a session with seventy-five of the most senior women at a Fortune 100 company. The women took the "Cultural Values Profile" we offer at the Cultural Intelligence Center—an inventory that measures cultural value preferences like the ones we just described (direct versus indirect, individualist versus collectivist, etc.). Typically this tool reveals a range of diversity in cultural values, even if the team appears relatively homogenous. The women were from all over the world, yet they were remarkably similar in almost all their cultural values. All seventy-five were direct communicators, competitive, and task-oriented. I asked our team to double check the group profile because it seemed unlikely that seventy-five women from across the globe were scoring identically on many of the dimensions.

When I shared the results with the women, they weren't the least bit surprised. They said, "How do you think we ended up in these positions? We wouldn't be here if we didn't think and work like the guys upstairs." Were they selling out? Or were they adapting to survive? This is a tough question. Authenticity is the holy grail of diversity efforts: *Bring your whole self to work.* Yet adapting to the preferences of others is at the core of cultural intelligence. How do we give people the safety to be themselves while also expecting flexibility as a "team player"? And when do an organization's values unify, and when do they squelch diversity and innovation?

Being true to oneself is a critical value that has been proven to have an impact on employee well-being and engagement. My concern is when authenticity becomes an excuse for inflexibility. The more you work with people from different worlds, the more you have to choose between what is effective for your counterparts and what feels authentic to you. What's "authentic" for me may be "offensive" for you.

Did the women from the Fortune 100 company sell out? It depends. Everyone has to regulate how much of themselves to reveal and uncover based on the context and the objective. Many of these women sacrificed the freedom to lead with complete authenticity. But by being willing to adapt to the dominant culture, they succeeded in their own careers and created room for other women to lead. Their willingness to adapt to the dominant norms may have given them some new perspectives and values they wouldn't have gained if they had insisted on doing things their way. Any individual or organization can adapt too far and lose themselves in the process. But some adaptation is almost always necessary.

Here are a few questions to consider when thinking about how to adapt the way we present ourselves at work:

+ *Is this a tight or loose world?* Tight worlds have strong social norms and view deviation from those norms suspiciously, and adapting to them often leads to a better social outcome. Loose worlds might view it as ridiculous for someone to adapt.
+ *What is my objective?* My goal in China was to show my humanity and demonstrate how to learn from failure. So, the question becomes, what is the best way to accomplish that goal in this context? A robotic approach says *A self-effacing story is the way to show I'm human.* A culturally intelligent approach knows there are multiple ways to show my humanity, such as waiting until later in the presentation to mention a failure or sharing something about my family to humanize my presentation.
+ *Will adapting compromise the core of who I am?* There are some norms I'm unwilling to accommodate, either because they go against my core convictions or force me to no longer be true to myself. But instead of robotically aborting the behavior outright, a culturally intelligent approach stops to consider if it's truly core or merely a preference.

Making Sense of Problems

One more way culturally intelligent humans stand apart from robots is by adapting how we approach reasoning and logic. The World Economic Forum (WEF) predicts that analytical thinking, active learning, complex problem-solving, critical thinking, and creativity are the top-five job skills needed over the next decade.[7] Machines outpace humans when it comes to rapidly and efficiently analyzing data. But complex problems that require reasoning and logic need human brains. The more diversity involved, the harder it is to reason through things. When done well, however, diverse teams come up with a more complex understanding of a problem than either robots or homogenous teams.

Anytime you say, "That makes no sense," add the words "to me." Nearly every perspective makes sense to the person who has it. INSEAD University professor Erin Meyer contrasts a principles-first approach to reasoning versus an applications-first approach. Principles-first reasoning uses deductive logic. You spend time defining a problem, describing the theoretical process for addressing it, and eventually arrive at a conclusion. Applications-first reasoning uses inductive logic. You get to the point quickly and briefly reference the process used to get to the outcome. "Why" is less important than "how."[8]

When I'm presenting to most North American groups, I get to practical solutions as quickly as possible. A long explanation about the theoretical process of how we conceptualized and researched CQ is sure to be met with impatience. *Just get to the bottom line!* If I'm making a presentation about cultural intelligence in Europe, however, I'll methodically walk through the process of how we conceptualized cultural intelligence, the design behind the CQ assessment, and eventually the conclusions reached. If I move too quickly to practical solutions, I'll be met with skepticism. *How did you arrive at this conclusion? What were the questions you started with?* It's not adequate to say, "We used sound, research methodology" (Figure 6.1).

These differences in reasoning exist in many other worlds too. Academics usually respect a principles-first approach more than an applications-first. My amazing editor Anna Leinberger and I debated this issue when we first started working on the structure for this book. I thought it was important to give readers a thorough understanding of

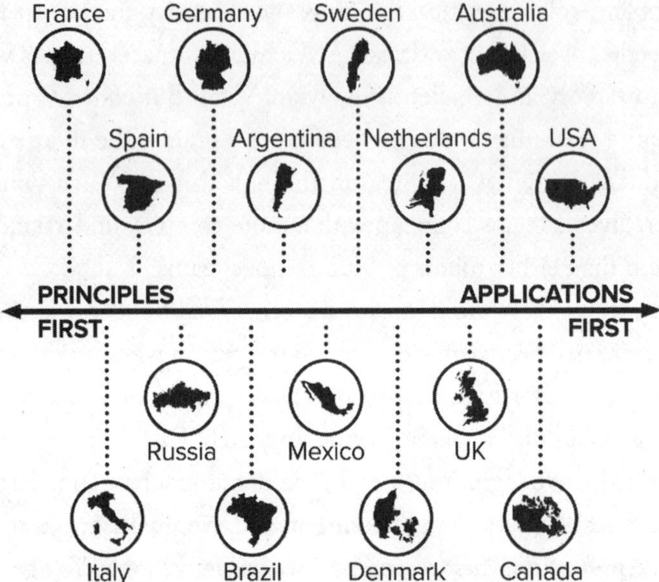

FIGURE 6.1 Principles-first versus applications-first cultures
By Cultural Intelligence Center, used with permission

CQ and different figured worlds before getting to the "how." Anna was concerned readers would be frustrated if they had to sit through too many chapters laying out concepts before they got to practical solutions. The diverse ways we use our brains to approach problems and solutions is a powerful way to contribute something that robots can't.

Culturally Intelligent Problem-Solving

Working with people from diverse worlds is almost always more challenging than working with people from similar backgrounds. Here are a few ways cultural intelligence helps us bridge divides in ways that robots can't.

Identify a Common Problem

The first step for bridging polarization at work begins with using CQ Drive to find a problem we're motivated to solve together. Problem identification is essential. We can't skip it. Whether it's a macro problem like Covid-19, climate change, or economic growth, or a more personalized issue like how to talk with a colleague about whether their comment was a racial microaggression, it's impossible to bridge our different worlds until we agree on a problem we care about.

Robots can help us with problem-solving. Algorithms and sophisticated technology have become very good at developing solutions more efficiently and accurately than humans. But where culturally intelligent humans are needed is in identifying the problem in the first place, particularly if it's a problem that hasn't happened before and can't be identified by running an automated diagnostic. Zooming out to a problem shared by a diverse group motivates the team to work together and help clarify the objective.

Problem finding isn't as simple as robotically stating the problem at the beginning of a project and moving on. Nor can you just go around the room and ask everyone if they understand the problem. Power dynamics, personality differences, and social norms cloud getting clarity. A culturally intelligent approach uses a more creative way to identify problems and ensure alignment. Ask individuals to independently write down a one-sentence description of the problem as they see it. What would successfully solving this problem look like to them? What would failure look like? Then curate the responses. Pay as much attention to the differences as to the recurring themes that emerge. See if you can reach consensus on what the problem is. Don't rush through this. This simple but deliberate practice of zooming out to a problem we agree on can make a world of difference.

Understand Perceived Causes and Solutions for the Problem

Once you agree on the problem, use CQ Knowledge to zoom back in to understand different explanations for the problem. Compare the different perceptions of the root causes and try explaining your perspective in the third-person. This gives you some emotional distance from your point of view. Then try explaining your counterparts' views in the first-person as a way of internalizing their values and assumptions. Anytime you catch the slightest bit of overlap, write it down. Give equal attention to the power of your differences to address the problem. For example, a group that is more oriented toward the long-term impact of everyone working remotely needs the input of more short-term oriented teammates who may highlight the immediate repercussions of empty offices and isolated team members.

Diversity by itself does not lead to innovation. We've studied dozens of multicultural teams around the world, and more often than not, homogeneous teams come up with *more* innovative solutions than diverse teams do. Homogeneous teams easily agree on the problem and use similar approaches for solving it. But when diverse teams have high CQ, they far outpace homogenous teams in coming up with more innovative solutions. Cultural intelligence allows them to use their differences as a source of human analysis and creativity.[9]

A Pakistani woman living in Liverpool, England, repeatedly told her doctor that her heart hurt. The physician ran a battery of tests including x-rays, an EKG, blood work, and stress tests. Everything came back showing her heart was healthy, but she insisted it hurt. The physician talked with a cardiologist who robotically ran additional tests, and together the doctors concluded it was all in her head. They told the woman she had nothing to worry about. When she committed suicide a few months later, it dawned on the doctors that the she had been trying to tell them that she was riddled with anxiety and depression. Not only were there no words in her native language to describe depression, she was embarrassed to talk about it given the shame her world associated with mental illness. Failure to understand the root cause of the problem cost the woman her life.

Innovative solutions to problems stem from many different ways to analyze the problem. Some perspectives will focus more on causes and others more on the solutions but together the diverse perspectives lead to a richer analysis than anything you get from an automated or homogeneous analysis.[10] Zoom up-close on the different views of a problem and work hard to understand the different perspectives. Robots work faster and more efficiently. But the problems that polarize us require a more complex understanding of the differences.

Develop Third-Way Solutions That Require Resources and Commitment from Diverse Worlds

The next step is to use CQ Strategy to design a solution to the shared problem. This step requires mid-range focus. We need to zoom wide enough to transcend our differences but close enough to provide an incentive for everyone to be invested in solving the problem together. The strategic problem-solving capabilities we gain from CQ Strategy are critical for doing something about the problem we have in common.

Problem-solving with people who disagree usually defaults to winners versus losers or to a vanilla "agree to disagree" approach. But that won't resolve most of the challenges facing us, nor will it do anything to reduce polarization. We have to keep pushing through the differences to find third-way solutions that only work if we're all in on them. This might mean employing something like the "five whys" approach originated by Toyota as a way of analyzing a problem beneath the surface.

Here's an example: People refuse to get vaccinated.

Why—Because they don't trust the vaccine.

Why—Because they think Covid-19 is a political ploy.

Why—Because they believe the government keeps taking away their rights.

Why—Because the government thinks they can do a better job of protecting us.

Why—Because so many people are dying from Covid.

"So many people are dying from Covid." That's a problem many can agree on. So the solution needs to stay focused on how to address the problem of so many people dying from Covid. This links back to ensuring we identified the right problem in the first place. Then we can begin to figure out a solution that requires something from all of us.

At the Cultural Intelligence Center we, like many organizations, had to decide if and how to bring people back to the office following the extended work-from-home period during the Covid-19 pandemic. Our team represents a wide spectrum of opinions about vaccines, remote working, and risk tolerance. We agreed on the common problem—keeping people safe while ensuring productivity and effectiveness. We were pretty clear about the vastly different perspectives among us—trust people to do what's best versus mandate vaccines to ensure the greater good—but we kept getting stalled there. We had to set aside our debates and become very explicit about what decisions needed to be made, the process we would use for making the decision, and how we would communicate the decision as a united front. We eventually ended up with a solution that we believe was inclusive, equitable, and unifying where vaccination was required for in-person work. But it took time to get there.

Part of using CQ Strategy on a work team comes from creating more explicit processes for things like communication, roles, and decision-making. When everyone shares the same background, there's less need to be explicit about who does what, how to communicate, and the process for making decisions. By default, we know what to do. But these are practices that are deeply shaped by our figured worlds. The strategies for effectively solving problems with diverse groups aren't rocket science. They include pretty basic things like creating explicit guidelines for email communication, how to address conflict, how to classify decisions, and outlining the purpose for a meeting. But it's remarkable how often we overlook taking the time to consciously use these relatively simple practices. An explicit process and solution is a more effective way of including and empowering everyone to adapt as needed in the midst of changing circumstances rather than robotically enforcing an inflexible process.

Implement Solutions with the Support of Leadership and Resources

It's show time! Implementation of a collaborative solution requires actively adjusting our focus and behavior in the moment, which is where CQ Action comes in. This takes all of us. Schools need principals and deans who forge relationships with faculty, students, and staff from different disciplines, ideologies, and backgrounds. Churches, temples, and mosques need religious leaders who inspire police officers, diverse families, Republicans, and Democrats to use their vastly different views to improve the way they pursue their faith and mission. Companies needs CEOs, vice presidents, and mid-level managers who actively solicit and support the contributions of trans individuals, millennials, old white guys, Black, brown, disabled, and every other kind of employee—not to meet diversity quotas, but to be workplaces that bring out the best of our humanity while improving the bottom line.

Stress, exhaustion, and roadblocks can quickly diminish the resolve to adapt to one another in the name of solving common problems. Any of us may need to step away from the work periodically to replenish our physical and emotional reserves. The most important resource to ensure continued collaboration and adaptation to overcome our polarized divides is leadership that provides the vision and resources to help us actively implement solutions.

Consciously apply your diversity to develop innovative solutions. This is one of the great values of diversity. Had the medical team caring for the Pakistani woman included individuals from South Asia, they may have more quickly determined that her problem wasn't cardio-related.

Amazon repeatedly promotes the importance of an empty chair at key leadership meetings to represent the customer. The more diversity you have sitting around the table, the better your understanding will be of the diversity of customers, students, or patients represented by that empty chair, as long as you consciously hear, consider, and use the diverse perspectives represented.

Help Wanted!

Robots can't become human. But without CQ, humans run the risk of becoming like robots. A culturally intelligent, human approach gives us an adaptability that robots don't have. Look at the marketing algorithms that curate ads to you. Sometimes they're surprisingly accurate, but other times they're completely off. There's no substitute for humans understanding and adapting to other humans.

The World Economic Forum predicts a loss of 85 million jobs to robots over a four-year period. However, 97 million new jobs will be needed to facilitate adapting to the realities of the twenty-first-century world. These new jobs are largely focused on the ability to apply knowledge and data to solve complex problems that increasingly polarize us.[11] Emotional intelligence is one of the critical skills needed to do this; organizations need staff who are adept at reading and managing the emotions of themselves and others. But emotional intelligence doesn't predict your ability to work and relate with people from different backgrounds. Cultural intelligence does. It picks up where emotional intelligence leaves off by providing the agility to work and relate effectively with a diversity of people to solve problems that matter to all of us.

In the words of Darwin: "It's not the strongest that survives, not the most intelligent. It's the one that is most adaptable to change."

PART III

CQ Solutions for Polarized Worlds

Polarization will continue to accelerate unless we reclaim our humanity by applying cultural intelligence to the figured worlds where we live. All of us are part of many figured worlds, but I'm going to address five that are at the center of our colliding perspectives: place, race, gender, faith, and politics. These aren't the only worlds that divide us, but if we can bridge the differences from these worlds, we'll be well on our way to overcoming the polarization that shows up everywhere we turn.

In each figured world, we'll apply the four CQ competences for working across our differences:

+ CQ Drive gives us the motivation to zoom wider than our differences to find a common problem.
+ CQ Knowledge helps us zoom back in on our differences to understand the root causes of the problem.
+ CQ Strategy provides a mid-range focus to plan practical solutions that address common problems together.

+ CQ Action enables us to actively adjust our focus in the moment to implement collaborative solutions.

In the real world we don't always use the four CQ competencies in a linear order (CQ Drive, Knowledge, Strategy, and Action). Instead, we draw upon them as needed. You'll see how this works throughout these chapters. As we apply cultural intelligence to the worlds that divide us, we can make *the whole wide world* a better place for all of us.

SEVEN

Place

Akifa, a department head at a university in Toronto, got funding for an app that would be used for a global innovation competition. She put out a request for proposal (RFP) to find a vendor to create the app, and after reviewing the proposals, she recommended the university award the contract to a Manila-based firm. Akifa and a committee reviewed their work, talked to their references, and noted that their price was 40 percent less than the other top contenders.

But the university was concerned about awarding the contract to a Filipino firm and asked Akifa to find a US or Canadian firm to ensure quality. Akifa asked her colleague Katie for help; Katie was also on the committee that reviewed the proposals, and she too thought the Filipino firm was the best option. She and Akifa went to the administration together, and Katie told them the same thing: "The Filipino firm is not only cheaper, they're more responsive and their quality is equivalent with the top North American contenders." With Katie's endorsement the administration not only awarded the contract to the Manila-based firm, they hired them for some other software projects, saving the university thousands of dollars.

Why did the university trust Katie and not Akifa? Was it just a matter of their persuasive abilities, or were colliding worlds at play? There's compelling evidence that "place" played a significant part in why the university was reluctant to trust a firm on the other side of the world, recommended by someone who looks like Akifa.

Where are you from? For people like Katie, it's a relatively easy question. She grew up in the same house in Grand Rapids, Michigan, until she left for college. Her parents still live there, and nearly all their extended family are nearby. Katie and her husband now live with their two young kids in Toronto, but Michigan is still the first place she thinks of as home. For people like Akifa, however, the idea of "home" is more complicated. She was born in Khartoum, Sudan. Her family moved to Qatar when she was two, she went to university in the UK, and she now lives with her Filipino husband and kids in Toronto. Each place is a part of home for Akifa and affects whom she trusts and why.

Place and our ideas of home can be polarizing because we decide who we can trust based on where they are from. We're suspicious of people from different places. Not everyone, everywhere, but our immediate impulse when faced with someone from an unfamiliar place is flight or fight. This can happen when someone in Indianapolis hears they're getting a new boss from San Francisco, or when someone in India learns they'll now report to Hong Kong. Building trust with colleagues and friends from different places requires cultural intelligence to work on problems we all care about.

The Power of Place

Katie left Michigan to attend Boston College before eventually accepting a job at a university in Toronto, where she met her husband. When I talked with Katie, she referred to both Grand Rapids and Toronto as home. At one point she said, "When I go home to see my parents…," and a minute later she said, "But this is definitely home now. We bought a house here, and I've even applied for Canadian citizenship."

Westerners treat the idea of home fluidly. We say, "Home is where the heart is." We might feel nostalgic about where we grew up, but our identity is not as strongly linked to geography. Only 13 percent of Australians, 21 percent of Canadians, and 32 percent of Americans say that where they were born is extremely important to them.[1] But for many people around the world, home isn't just where you are, it's *who* you are and the people you trust.

Akifa's parents were among thousands of Sudanese who migrated to Qatar for better paying jobs. Akifa's dad got a government job in the energy sector that paid ten times as much as he earned in Khartoum. But home was always Sudan. They sent money back to Sudan every month, and at least once a year they spent a month there. Growing up, Akifa remembers her mother crying a lot. She longed for the smells and sounds of the Nile River, and desperately wanted to hold her nieces and nephews. The moon seemed like the only thing Qatar and Sudan had in common, so she stared at it every night.

You don't have to leave your country to experience the power of place. Johannesburg versus Cape Town, Shanghai versus Beijing, Mumbai versus Delhi, Galway versus Dublin—regional rivalries exist all over the world. New York and San Francisco both view Los Angeles as their rival, but when Angelenos are asked about either city, they respond, "Great place! I love to visit!" But one New Yorker says, "Angelenos say they don't spend time comparing LA to New York in that same way people say they're totally over their exes." An Angeleno responded: "This just confirms how little New Yorkers understand us. If any city is *totally* over their exes, it's LA. We invented *Divorce Court*."

People in Ohio, Texas, and Wyoming find it laughable that New York and LA are different. To them, New Yorkers and Angelenos are just variations of the same untrustworthy, coastal elites. "Real America is in the heartland!" Cities and regions in the same country can be worlds apart.

The values that shape a place don't change quickly. Boston and San Francisco are both liberal, highly educated coastal cities with an emphasis on research, medicine, and venture capital. But their drastically different histories continue to shape these places. Boston started as the epicenter of Puritanism and to this day the city emphasizes tradition, status, and community. San Francisco emerged with the Gold Rush and emphasizes opportunity, egalitarianism, and innovation. Harvard markets a "tradition of excellence." Stanford describes itself as "free from the boundaries of tradition."[2] What do you trust more—tradition or innovation?

If you've ever felt disoriented moving from one place to another, it's because you're experiencing culture shock. Place shapes us at a fundamental level, and we experience those profound differences when we decide whether to trust colleagues and friends online, at the office, and in our neighborhoods.

Through the Eyes of Place

How does place shape whom we trust and why? Neeraj Garg, CEO of Coke India, says many Westerners never earn trust with colleagues or suppliers in India because they get down to business too quickly. For many South Asians friendly conversations over coffee or tea are a critical part of establishing the cognitive and social trust needed to work together effectively. The reverse is true in many Western contexts. Too much time spent socializing can feel like a waste of time and erode trust.

Cognitive Trust

Katie was incensed that the university administrators never apologized to Akifa for questioning her recommendation. Akifa told her to let it go. For her the fact that they not only eventually went with the Filipino firm but also hired them for additional work was enough. The university's reluctance to trust her and the Manila-based firm is not uncommon. It's easier to cognitively trust the capabilities of people who come from similar places. And this works both ways. Not only are Germans more likely to trust Germans, Chinese are more likely to trust Chinese. One study revealed that Chinese workers consistently describe their expat managers as empty vessels—all talk and no content. One Chinese worker described his expat manager saying, "I mean, he has no knowledge in this industry, and he told something, to me it's very stupid…he's just talking, talking."[3]

Our impulse to distrust people from different places can be triggered the minute we hear someone talk. One survey found that US passengers trust a pilot with a Southern accent significantly less than one with a Midwestern accent.[4] Whether you say "y'all" has nothing to do with your capability to fly a plane, but we're predisposed to question the capabilities of people from certain places. Even babies gravitate toward people from the same place. In one study, researchers offered two equally attractive toys to a group of American and French ten-month-olds. One toy was offered by an English-speaking adult and the other by a French-speaking adult. The babies consistently reached for the toy offered by the adult from their place.[5]

Our homes teach us unspoken rules about how to restore trust when it's broken. And in the digital age, companies are expected to get on top of rebuilding trust immediately. When gas pedals were allegedly getting stuck in hundreds of Toyotas, CEO Akio Toyoda made multiple public apologies. Toyota took out full-page ads that said: "We apologize from the bottom of our hearts for the great inconvenience and worries that we have caused you all." Similar scandals in the US and Europe come with more lukewarm apologies. After the oil spill in the Gulf of Mexico, BP's CEO Tony Hayward said: "We're sorry for the massive disruption it's caused. There's no one who wants this over more than I do. *I'd like my life back.*"

Westerners associate apologies with guilt and use them to assign blame. Responsibility is typically attributed to an individual. And in the digital world the words of an apology live on forever. In Japan, however, responsibility is shared. An expression of general remorse does not necessarily imply blame or responsibility. You rebuild trust by apologizing for the disruption of harmony.[6]

In a work setting, reliability and follow-through are critical for building trust with me. Send me a quick email to keep me updated and I'm content. But for others, detailed analysis, the approach used to complete a project, and regular times to chat about it might be more important for building cognitive trust.

Social Trust

Another critical form of trust is social trust, which is whether we trust others to treat us right. This comes through in whether someone is polite and demonstrates care for our feelings. When Katie left Michigan to go to school in Boston, the first thing that struck her was how rude people were. Even the baristas at the campus coffee shop were abrupt. People in Grand Rapids couldn't be nicer. It's where I lived for several years, and it epitomizes Midwest values—conservative politically, strong work ethic, high priority on family, extremely religious, and a whole lot of "Midwest nice." Katie's observation about rude East Coasters is something many people from smaller cities observe when they go to large urban areas. But think about it. If you stop to chat with every customer at a busy bagel shop in New York or Boston, you'll never keep up. And a continual pattern of relating this way reinforces this kind of behavior, even if on occasion there's only one customer in the shop.

Observe the differences in colleagues' and friends' preferences for small talk. Beginning an email abruptly with someone from Brazil may come off as rude or cold. But starting a virtual meeting talking about the weather can be perceived as a waste of time for someone from Germany or New York. I'm making some very broad generalizations. Many Brazilians would be fine with a task-only email, and there are Germans and New Yorkers who would be okay starting a meeting with small talk. But applying cultural intelligence to the chasm of trust includes using CQ Knowledge to understand how manners, professional etiquette, and respect are deeply shaped by the places we come from.

There are other dimensions of trust, but my point is, the values and perspectives instilled in us from the places we call home profoundly shape how we live and work together. Ask colleagues from different places about how the following factors influence whether they perceive a teammate is trustworthy: punctuality, warmth, reputation, character, results. You might be surprised at the differences.

CQ Solutions

Working together to address a common problem is one of the most effective ways to build trust among people from different places. In a work setting, identifying common problems comes pretty naturally—getting a drug to market, revising the eighth-grade curriculum, or achieving the next quarter's sales targets. But we easily lose sight of those objectives when a colleague from a different place communicates to us in a way that seems rude and disrespectful.

CQ Drive give us the motivation to zoom wider than the irritating differences so that we can see each other's humanity and focus on solving a problem we both care about. With CQ Knowledge we can zoom back in to see whether the behavior is in fact disrespectful or simply a difference that emerges from our unique backgrounds and preferences. And an enhanced understanding of our differences can help us analyze a problem more fully. With CQ Strategy we establish norms for how to communicate effectively and develop a plan for solving the problem together. And with CQ Action we can actively adapt to the norms we've developed.

But let's get more specific. Here are some ways to use cultural intelligence to bridge the divides among people from different places.

Improvise Expectations

Is a trustworthy coffee shop one that efficiently takes orders and serves great coffee? Or is it a place where they know your name and chat with you about your day? As Katie shifted her expectations about the kind of service to expect in places like Boston and Toronto, it reduced her tendency to view abrupt service as rude, and it helped her develop the CQ Drive to appreciate and even respect the different approach.

The challenge is our expectations run deep. The places we live create unspoken impressions in our heads that become the standard by which we evaluate others. A Danish woman who sees a Chinese man butting ahead in line thinks, *He just doesn't care about good manners.* A Chinese man who hears a Danish woman decline an invitation to a business dinner thinks, *She just doesn't care about good manners.* These momentary encounters get applied to other people from these places. But what if we slowed down from immediately evaluating others' trustworthiness in light of our expectations and applied CQ Knowledge to consider whether a colleague from another place is operating from a different set of codes than we are? When you work with a colleague from a different place, compare expectations around things like:

+ What is the biggest thing that erodes your trust in a colleague? Friend?
+ What do you value more in email communication—warmth or brevity?
+ What do you mean by "now" (e.g., as in "I'm finishing this up 'now.'")?

Akifa assumed her Sudanese background combined with being married to a Filipino played a role in the university's hesitancy to trust her recommendation to hire the Filipino tech company. In her younger years she would have confronted the bias head on: "No. This isn't my in-laws' company!" But after a lifetime of negotiating the places she calls home, Akifa's primary objective today is to improvise her expectations of others to facilitate what needs to get done. Her priority was seeing this project move forward and awarding the business to a company that would do the best job. She improvised her expectations from trying to manage the biases of the administration and leveraged her relationship with Katie to get the recommendation supported. "Some might say I sold out," Akifa said. "In my mind, the best way to confront their bias about their capabilities was to let them gain firsthand experience with the great work that could be done by an overseas vendor." She used her CQ Knowledge to consider the key trust factors for people who come from different places. She used her CQ Strategy to develop a plan that she believes will be effective.

Akifa's flexibility and self-awareness are a great example of how to bridge the chasm of trust across different places. But Akifa and Katie may have been able to apply CQ Strategy even further by clarifying the administration's expectations upfront. They assumed cost was a top priority, but the administration was more concerned about reliability and easy access to the vendor. It also would have been helpful to know upfront whether the university was open to using overseas providers. Explicitly defining the expectations would have provided clarity for Akifa and her committee, and it would have helped them make a stronger recommendation in light of the university's stated priorities.

Solve Problems Together

I met Akifa and Katie when I visited the university where they both teach. Their friendship began through a shared interest in Sudan. Katie's family fostered two Sudanese boys when she was in middle school. Both women talk to many Sudanese students on campus who wrestle with what it means to be Sudanese. Many of them haven't lived in Sudan since they were toddlers. In fact, the students have grown up in different places all over the world, but Sudan is a part of "home" for them. It doesn't take long, however, for the students' trust in each other to dissipate.

The Sudanese students who grew up in North America talk, eat, and dress differently than those who grew up in the Middle East or Africa. Passing references to pop culture and the North American students' more liberal views about sexuality, gender roles, and capitalism reveal the vastly different places they come from. This is true regardless of whether the students are from Christian or Muslim families. Katie sees this as a rich opportunity for dialogue and debate; it's more unnerving for Akifa, who empathizes with how disorienting it is for the students who grew up in different places.

Akifa and Katie decided to create a campus group focused on Sudan. They organized discussions around current events in Sudan, but the conversations inevitably evolved into polarizing debates about whether the Sudanese government was corrupt, the prevalence of sexual harassment, and whether Sudan should become one nation again. At first, Akifa and Katie decided to follow the students' conversations. They spent a whole evening debating whether Sudanese men should shake hands with a woman as part of an internship interview in Toronto, and another evening arguing whether women are responsible for being harassed because of how they dress. The places we come from intersect with other figured worlds like faith and gender.

Akifa and Katie were discouraged. What was intended to unite students with a tie to Sudan was instead polarizing them. It wasn't that a Sudanese student from Nairobi consciously distrusted a peer from Minneapolis. But their divergent values and ideas followed geographical lines, which resulted in in-groups and out-groups. Akifa and Katie challenged the students to zoom wider than their differences and focus on a problem that mattered to all of them—the economic growth and development of Sudan.

Akifa and Katie led several brainstorming sessions about how the group could actively support economic development in Sudan. But most of the ideas came from the students who grew up in the West, where brainstorming and discussion were comfortable and familiar. Meanwhile, a few students from other places dominated discussions with long monologues that continually repeated the same points over and over. Brainstorming might seem ideally suited for diverse groups, but it's a technique that is biased toward individualists who enjoy raising independent, divergent ideas. People who grew up in collectivist places like Kenya, Sudan, or Qatar tend to prioritize harmony, conformity, and not standing out with a unique idea, ideas that go directly against the brainstorming approach.

Akifa and Katie augmented their approach again, an important part of applying cultural intelligence. We almost never get it right the first time; we have to continue to read the cues and use CQ Action to adjust the approach. They adapted the brainstorming sessions by having the students write down as many ideas as possible before anyone spoke up. Then they asked each person to share one idea. This method allowed less vocal group members to have their contributions considered alongside the ideas of those who readily speak up. In addition, Akifa and Katie began to group students according to their academic majors and told them to reach consensus on two or three specific ways to support the economic development of Sudan. Business students who grew up in Montreal, Doha, and Khartoum suddenly bonded by using their similar expertise and language from their business classes. The same was true for students who shared majors in education, psychology, or international studies. They found a common identity in their academic interests that transcended the differences from where they grew up.

Akifa and Katie's perseverance resulted in the students' idea for the app that would facilitate a global innovation competition. The winning team would receive a grant to support the most innovative approach to leveraging the resources of Sudan to build a more sustainable economy. The Sudanese group discovered a shared identity that, while centered around Sudan, was actually comprised of many different places. By deciding to focus on one concrete solution they could pursue together, they transcended their ideological differences. This led to something with the potential to make a real difference in Sudan, and the students found a wider network of friends.

Time Travel

One more way cultural intelligence can bridge the trust gap between places is to use what Ethan Kross, author of the book *Chatter,* calls mental time travel. This is when you mentally fast-forward to gain perspective on something that is upsetting you in the moment. "Think about how you'll feel a month, a year, or even longer from now," Kross writes. "Remind yourself that you'll look back on whatever it is upsetting you in the future and it'll seem much less upsetting."[7] Mental time travel highlights the impermanence of our current reality. It's a way to use CQ Strategy by being mindful and aware.

Mental time travel helps you deal with the irritation and distrust of someone cutting ahead of you in line or talking too much in a meeting. Fast-forward twenty-four hours and you can see that this frustration isn't worth much mental energy. But how do you use time travel to solve the more polarizing issues between places?

Once the Sudanese students agreed on creating an app, Akifa and Katie asked them to imagine they're five years in the future. *The app was a raving success. What would look different in Sudan five years from now as a result?* Then they asked them to do the reverse. *Imagine that in five years the app is a complete failure. What were the causes for the failure?* Next, Katie and Akifa asked each student to find someone in the group who grew up in a different place than them, the more different the better. The pairs role-played how they hoped their kids would interact as university classmates in twenty-five years. The future orientation helped the group focus on their overarching goal. The more their conversation and energy was put on working to build a better Sudan, the less time they spent debating their differences.

Mental time travel is a strategy I regularly use to deal with the everyday challenges of working with people from different places. It's a way to manage stress and anxiety, and it helps keep trust focused on the key objective we're trying to accomplish together.

Finding Our Way Home

For almost everyone, where we grew up holds iconic status. We go back to visit, and it only takes a couple cues to immediately take us back to who we were when we lived there. The minute we meet someone from our hometown, we feel a connection. One of the reasons we often ask a new acquaintance "Where are you from?" is because it quickly tells us something important about them.[8]

Manila and Toronto seem worlds apart. But in the digital age, they're only a click away. As we work together with people from other places to solve common problems, we suddenly find ourselves at home in some of the most surprising places. Working together to address shared challenges leads to reciprocal, trusting relationships with people from all kinds of nations, regions, and cultures. That leads to a better world for all of us. But what if you're in the wrong place at the wrong time?

EIGHT

Race

The story of Philando Castille and Diamond Reynolds is tragically familiar. A Black couple drives through the suburbs with their four-year-old daughter and is pulled over for a routine traffic stop. A couple minutes later, Philando is dead, killed by a police officer who alleged Philando was drawing a weapon. Diamond captured the entire incident on her smartphone. After the video went viral on Facebook, filmmaker Luke Willis Thompson convinced Diamond to work with him to create a documentary. Thompson wasn't interested in sensationalizing the violence. Instead, he wanted to portray Diamond's beauty, fortitude, and dignity amid devastating loss and pain. The result was *Autoportrait*, an award-winning black-and-white documentary that consists of two four-minute takes of Diamond posing in a dark room.[1]

Thompson's film won the prestigious Turner Prize from the Tate Modern in London. The issues of injustice and discrimination are not foreign to him. As a mixed-race artist from Fiji, Thompson understands what it's like to be colonized by another race. It's not adjacent to being Black in America, but it gives him a spirit of resonance. Not everyone agrees, however. Black artist René Matic says that Thompson's work exploits Black suffering. She doesn't think these are his stories to share. He's a white-passing male who cannot possibly understand Diamond Reynolds's day-to-day experience as a Black woman.[2]

Race is polarizing because there is vehement disagreement about whether race has any bearing on how someone is treated. Should universities and employers intentionally recruit applicants from specific racial groups, or is that perpetuating the problem? Does law enforcement have a problem with racism, or are there just a few bad apples? And are artists like Thompson too white to make films about Black people? We can get live pictures from Mars, develop vaccines for a deadly virus, and create self-driving cars, but we can't seem to get beyond the color of our skin. Cultural intelligence is a critical tool for addressing the complicated divisions surrounding race.

The Power of Race

It's impossible to understand the power of race apart from economics and power. Race was created to justify colonization and slavery in the interest of economic advancement and control. Yet many argue that economic opportunity is the best way to address racial injustice. Swedish economists Nicolas Berggren and Therese Nilsson hypothesized that market-based economies have higher levels of tolerance. They measured the links between economic opportunity and racial tolerance in sixty-nine countries. Their research was fresh in my mind when I met Mei, Pari, and Nazra, three undergraduates at the National University of Singapore. Singapore, one of the countries included in Berggren and Nilsson's study, skyrocketed to be one of the world's most robust economies in record time. The island republic was founded on the idea of learning to live together in racial harmony.

Mei, Pari, and Nazra met as first-year university students. After being in multiple business courses together, they became friends and decided to live together. Like most Singaporeans, they love to shop, eat amazing food, and they take their studies seriously. They're also a picture of

Singapore's ethnic diversity. Mei is Chinese, Pari is Indian, and Nazra is Malay, but they're all Singaporean.

A professor arranged for me to have lunch with Mei, Pari, and Nazra following a lecture I gave on campus. They wanted to interview me for a project, and I had a few questions for them. After more than twenty years of working in Singapore, my perception is that multiracial relationships among Singaporeans are pleasant but somewhat peripheral—neighbors, coworkers, and classmates greet one another and have occasional conversations, but they mostly stick with people like themselves. So I was intrigued by the special friendship between these young women coming from the three primary ethnic groups in Singapore, which is about 74 percent Chinese, 13 percent Malay, and 9 percent Indian.

I asked the students how they would describe racism in Singapore. Pari spoke up first. "Singapore is a racially harmonious place. It's one of the things that is so unique about it. The only thing the West thinks about Singapore is that you get caned for chewing gum." Mei and Nazra giggled, and Nazra added: "And they think we're all crazy rich Asians." But I knew that Malays sometimes feel like second-class citizens in Singapore. I turned to Nazra and asked, "Do you think most Malays believe Singapore is racially harmonious?" She said, "Oh yes. I mean, are there jokes about the different ethnic groups? Sure. But we're not overly sensitive about racial issues like Americans. People just say what they think."

Berggren and Nilsson found no evidence to support the premise that prosperous countries like Singapore are more tolerant.[3] In fact, the same issues of discrimination that occur in companies around the world happen in Singapore. Malay applicants with identical qualifications as Chinese are consistently viewed as less competent and qualified.[4] And when a recent advertisement for e-payments featured a Chinese actor who used brownface and stereotypical accents to portray Malay and Indian customers, social media lit up with outrage.[5] Race is always lurking beneath the surface in what we see and how we experience the world.

Economic development is an important factor, but it's not enough to bridge our racial divides.

Racial categories are held in place by cultural, political, ideological, and legal functions in nearly every society across the world and that affects our interpersonal interactions. It's not that most police officers intend to single out people of color. But when a police officer has to justify their use of force, they carry the power and history of a legal system that consistently rules in their favor.[6] A great deal of the recent conversation about race has highlighted the driving influence of systemic racism, a codification of inequality in law, structures, public policies, school curriculum, and more.

One of the most familiar examples of systemic racism is redlining, when US government officials and banks drew lines around areas deemed poor financial risks due to the racial compositions of those neighborhoods. Banks subsequently refused to offer mortgages to the people in those areas, which were predominantly African Americans. We have to consider the role of systemic racism as a part of bridging racial divides interpersonally. There are dozens of books to help increase our CQ Knowledge about systemic racism. If this topic is new to you, start with *Between the World and Me* by Ta-Nehisi Coates or *An Indigenous Peoples' History of the United States* by Roxanne Dunbar-Ortiz.

Defining people by race and ethnicity is ingrained in the way societies are structured all over the world. But the greatest impact of race is the subtle but real correlations between race and inequality. Race is what is referred to as a "master status," which means one's access to resources is strongly predicted by race. Let's use health as an example. There's a significant disparity in the medical care that is accessible based on race. In the UK, for instance, Caribbean men are far less likely to have a general practitioner than white men are. In the US, Native Americans are much less likely to receive early diagnosis of a chronic disease than the majority of the US population. Across Eastern Europe, many Roma people are not registered in the national health care systems. And in Nepal, birth control is unavailable to Dalits. Even when controlling for income, education, and ability to pay, many physicians are more likely to spend more time diagnosing and providing treatment for white people than for people of color.[7]

If there's no biological difference between races, there must be some other explanation for these inequities. Similar statistics exist for educational and economic inequality. Many argue that we can shrug this off as being way more complicated than what meets the eye. But consider instead that we can start by acknowledging that if the only difference between two people is their race, and one of them has an advantage over the other, it must be because of how the system in which they operate is built. Race matters in real life because society decided it matters. It wields immense power in how societies work all over the world, but by acknowledging the power of race, we can slowly dismantle racism.

Through the Eyes of Race

Some of the ways race shapes our thinking and behavior are not very different from how nationality does so. The degree to which we prefer direct versus indirect communication, our preferred leadership style, or our time orientation can all be shaped by our racial background. But the more critical point to understand when looking at our racial identity is how differently it shapes the way we experience the world. People living next door to each other have very different experiences depending on their race.

Some argue that the reason race continues to be such a divisive issue is because we make it one—"Politicians and the media use identity politics to create artificial divides." There's some merit to this. Attention bias says that what we pay attention to shapes how we experience the world. So, if I'm constantly looking through the lens of race, it's going to shape how I interpret things. Likewise, if I dismiss race from having any bearing, it will have a direct impact on how I see myself and others.

Those of us who come from a dominant racial group have the hardest time seeing the relevance of race to our daily lives. Sociologist Karyn McKinney has done fascinating work on what it means to be white. When she tells other white people that she studies whiteness, many act congratulatory, as if to say, "Good for you! We've given enough attention to *them*; it's time some academic gave some attention to us."[8] McKinney asked her white students to write about their experience being white in the US. The students found the assignment exceptionally difficult. *What does being white even mean? It's not something I ever think about.* They wrote things like: "When I describe myself, white does not pop into my head. I guess this is because I was brought up in a family where race did not matter. Everyone is equal. We're all Americans."[9]

To some extent, many Chinese Singaporeans agree. They're the least likely group of Singaporeans to identify with their racial identity. In their view, "We're all Singaporeans." However, more than half of Malay Singaporeans think that being Malay is equally or more important than being Singaporean.[10] The more dominant your racial group, the less likely you are to be conscious of it. The perks of being white follow me around the world. This was one of the most alarming things for me as I began to travel internationally. I thought being the lone white person boarding a train in Delhi or walking the streets of Cairo would give me a better understanding of what it means to be a minority. But my minority status in these environments brought me more perks than discrimination. I walked into a five-star hotel in Delhi to enjoy the air-conditioned lobby for a few minutes, and no one questioned whether I was a paying guest (I wasn't). I had an economy ticket to fly from Cairo to Dubai, but the airport staff assumed I was in the wrong line and insisted I stand in the premium traveler queue.

I'm continually aware of how my experience as a white guy dressed in business attire shapes the way I am seen. But I could walk away from that consciousness tomorrow and very little would change for me. If you're from a marginalized racial group, you're forced to wonder at every turn whether race plays a part in how you're treated—including positive treatment. I never wonder whether I was invited to speak at an event because they needed a white guy. Most people of color are forced to reconcile their racial identity at an early age. It's not optional. For white people, it is.

Many people of color also talk about the tendency of white people to intellectualize conversations about race, demonstrating discomfort with anything that feels too emotional or boisterous. But the pain and discomfort that come with the conversation are essential to healing. Boston University's Ibram X. Kendi says that without pain there is no progress in bridging our racial divides.[11] CQ Drive helps us become more comfortable with uncomfortable conversations and gives us the motivation to use CQ Action for how we respond to the pain that ensues.

Some Americans are concerned that white people are being marginalized and too much preference is given to "diversity hires." But the evidence doesn't support this. The people sitting in positions of power across the US continue to be disproportionately white. The ten richest Americans are white. An overwhelming 95 percent of the directors of the top one hundred grossing movies are white. And despite recent growth in diversity at the top levels of the US government, military, congressional, and executive leadership in the US is more than 90 percent white.[12] People argue that race is irrelevant, and we should simply hire the most competent individuals. To that I ask, *Why are 90 percent of the most "competent" leaders white?* It would be wonderful if we could "just hire based on competency" and live in a world where "all lives matter." But given the realities of racial inequity, intentional effort is needed to honor the humanity in all of us.

CQ Solutions

What can we possibly do to confront a division that has so much sway on our twenty-first-century reality? Thankfully, the research on cultural intelligence offers insight on how to bridge our racial divides.

CQ Drive helps us manage the emotional, physical, and intellectual exhaustion that comes from addressing racial injustice. With CQ Knowledge we learn what language and behavior perpetuates divisions and discrimination. Those of us from dominant racial groups need to take responsibility to educate ourselves rather than leaning on marginalized racial groups to teach us things we can learn on our own from books, films, and other sources. With the help of CQ Strategy we become more conscious of how our interactions with someone from a different racial background may be interpreted in light of a long, historical context of racial interactions. CQ Action is needed by everyone but especially those from dominant racial groups who tend to expect others to adapt to them. Here are some more tangible ways to use CQ to bridge our racial divides.

Seeing Me through You

Nearly every workshop addressing diversity and racism begins with the importance of self-awareness. It can feel like such a weak response to something that destroys people's lives. Awareness isn't enough but it is a critical step in the process, followed by dialogue and collaborative problem-solving to use our differences surrounding race to build a better future.

Self-awareness doesn't happen in isolation. I need interaction with people from different racial backgrounds in order to become more aware of my own racial identity. The same is true for you. This reciprocal cycle of awareness is the first step to bridging our divides, a skill that relies upon CQ Strategy. Sociologist Charles Horton Cooley wrote: "I am not what I think I am. I am not what you think I am. *I am what I think you think I am.*"[13] Reread that quote and think about it for a minute.

I've adapted the Johari window of self-awareness (Figure 8.1) to show what reciprocal awareness looks like. This is an oversimplification because our awareness is always susceptible to our assumptions and biases. But it provides a starting point for using CQ Strategy to see each other more clearly.

WHAT I SEE	WHAT YOU SEE
My intentions; my perceptions of your behavior.	Your intentions; your perceptions of my behavior.
WHAT BOTH SEE	**WHAT NEITHER SEES**
What happened.	Each other's intention; X factors.

FIGURE 8.1 Racial awareness window
By Grace Livermore, used with permission

Tense conversation. One time I was facilitating a CQ certification course, and an African American woman asked me a question. I attempted to answer it, but my response didn't satisfy her. She kept asking for additional clarification. I felt like it was getting a bit tense. On her third or fourth attempt she raised her voice and shook her finger at me. I tried to lighten the mood and said, "Okay! Don't yell at me. I'm sorry I made you mad." She stopped and the whole room was dead silent. "Okay," she said. "Let's do culture right now. You're assuming I'm mad because I raised my voice. I grew up as one of eight kids and raising my voice was the only way I was heard. I'm not mad. I just get louder when I'm not understood. I'm sorry that makes you uncomfortable."

I had no way of knowing whether she was mad. She had no idea whether I was uncomfortable. But my perceptions of her and her perceptions of me shaped our interaction (Figure 8.2). I regret that I responded

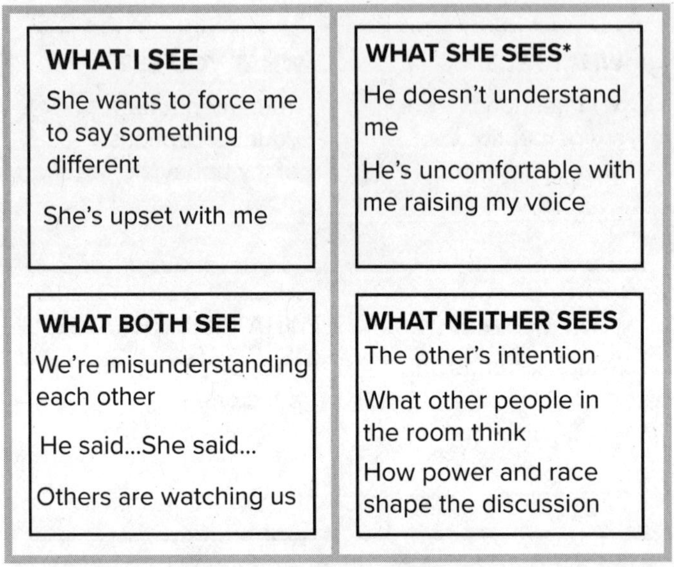

WHAT I SEE	**WHAT SHE SEES***
She wants to force me to say something different She's upset with me	He doesn't understand me He's uncomfortable with me raising my voice
WHAT BOTH SEE	**WHAT NEITHER SEES**
We're misunderstanding each other He said...She said... Others are watching us	The other's intention What other people in the room think How power and race shape the discussion

*I don't really know what she perceived because I'm not her. But using the power of perspective-taking, I at least have an educated guess about what she saw.

FIGURE 8.2 Racial awareness window—tense conversation
By Grace Livermore, used with permission

the way I did. But none of us ever do this perfectly. What happened next, however, began to bridge the divide. I acknowledged her point by saying, "In my house, raising your voice meant you were emotional and out-of-control. So you're right. I was using that same standard to evaluate your communication and I'm sorry. That wasn't fair or helpful." She immediately accepted my apology and we agreed to resume the conversation one-on-one at the next break. A while later, we reflected on our interaction and eventually discussed a project we were interested in doing together. Pursuing collaborative research further solidified our relationship. Mistakes are inevitable when crossing these divides. What's most important is that we acknowledge our mistakes, learn from them, and attempt to do better next time.

WHAT CAROL SEES	WHAT OTHERS SEE*
People are staring at me People aren't welcoming me	We've never seen her before There's a white woman here
WHAT ALL SEE	**WHAT NO ONE SEES**
How many white people are here? What actions occurred? Carol's friend welcomed and thanked her	What's most important to the grieving family? What biases influence Carol's perceptions and how she's perceived?

*We don't really know what the others perceived because we didn't hear from them.

FIGURE 8.3 Racial awareness window—reverse racism
By Grace Livermore, used with permission

Reverse racism. How does the window of racial awareness apply to the repeated claims that white people are victims of reverse racism? A white woman named Carol posted a comment on Black author Austin Channing Brown's blog about "nice white people." Carol wrote:

> Something black people need to recognize in themselves is a bit of prejudice against people with white skin....I shared an office with a wonderful girl. She and I were not the same age group, but in talking over the years we found we had much in common....The only difference we could find was the color of our skin, hers black and mine white.... Her father passed away....The wake was being held in her church.... Many of the folks were strangers to me but I smiled and said hello.... I could feel the stares. Like what is SHE doing here....Nobody was

mean, and they didn't try to chase me out, but neither were they very welcoming.

The online replies lit up. Austin Channing Brown responded by writing: "You went to a funeral, and you're upset that people didn't go out of their way to make you feel welcome...at a funeral...at a funeral."[14]

There are so many layers to Carol's comments. First, she needs to be aware that she's making an assumption about what welcoming behavior looks like. But let's assume she's right and the guests didn't appreciate her being there. If you feel like a whole system is organized against you by people who look like Carol, the skeptical, cold responses you're getting might have more to do with what you represent than whether you as an individual are a nice, nonracist, white person. Increased awareness makes us less susceptible to immediately interpreting these kinds of situations as a personal offense (Figure 8.3).

Redefine the "P" Word

A few weeks after meeting the Singaporean students, Puri sent me an email. She was reflecting on our conversation and specifically Mei. Puri wrote: "Mei is by far the most accepting of the three of us. She goes out of her way to include students who don't have friends and she treats her maid much better than most Singaporeans do. But the very fact that her family has a maid makes her different from Nazra and me." Laundry is one less thing Mei thinks about when she goes home for the weekend. And the fact that Mei's family goes to church with a couple of their professors makes her university experience different from Puri and Nazra's. Mei's school holidays inevitably include a quick jaunt to Bali or even a ski trip to France. Puri was looking for guidance on how to talk about these issues with Mei and Nazra.

Is Mei privileged? Are all Chinese Singaporeans privileged? Are all white people privileged? It depends how you define "privilege." Many middle-class people don't easily embrace the idea that they're privileged, much less those who are struggling to make ends meet. It's not like someone knocked on their door and handed them their college degree, job, and home. I would guess the same is true for Mei's family. They don't live in a bougie private condominium, and Mei's parents work long hours and always have.

Privilege exists on a spectrum. Who is more privileged? A white single mom living on welfare or an Indigenous married man with a professional job? Both have some privileges the other doesn't have. Skin color is one of the most significant variables of privilege, but there are others. Privilege is anything you are born into, not things you earned. Privilege has a direct impact on the opportunities you get. Having conversations about privilege is hard because people see things like a college degree or a promotion as something they've earned, which may be true, in part. But what cumulative advantages facilitated their opportunities along the way? For example, it may seem irrelevant to Mei that her family is friends with some of her professors. It's not like they're going to let her opt out of completing assignments or grade her on a curve. But she immediately gains what Harvard career adviser Gorick Ng calls a "guardian angel"; Mei enters university knowing powerful people who can introduce her to opportunities, help her navigate the university experience, and give her tips on how to succeed.[15]

Being in a position of privilege isn't something to be ashamed of. I can't strip away my privilege. But I'm conscious of how it changes the way I function in the world and the opportunities it affords my family. I broker introductions for my kids all the time. My daughter Emily was flying on Qatar Airlines, so I messaged a colleague who works there, and he ensured the crew gave her special attention all the way from Singapore to Cape Town. I've made similar introductions for my kids as they pursue degrees and jobs. They've worked hard in school and life, but my connections have eased the way for them.

If you are in a position of privilege, be mindful of the ways you can use privilege to level the playing field for others. Some ideas include:

+ Broker introductions. Privileged people have networks that include connections that can be the key to a less privileged person's opportunity.
+ Amplify marginalized voices. When a colleague's input is overlooked or talked over, use your voice to make sure they're heard and that their work is recognized.
+ Have tough conversations. The highly charged environment regarding racial differences can make privileged people fearful of saying anything about race. But that isn't helpful. Accept that you won't always get it right but make the effort to engage.

I encouraged Puri to avoid telling Mei she's privileged and instead to see if the three friends could reflect on the gradient of advantages they have. How would your life be different if you had been born a different gender? What about a different skin color? How would it change if you were a Malay in Singapore rather than Chinese, or what if you were a Bangladeshi foreign worker in Singapore? Unless we recognize one another's realities, we will never solve the problems we face. Someone is always more privileged than you. Someone is always less privileged than you.

Act Together

It's hard to think of a more extreme example of overcoming polarization than the friendship shared between Laurencia and Tasian, two Rwandan women who are next-door neighbors and friends. The women live in Mbyo, a tree-lined neighborhood an hour from Kigali. At the height of the Rwandan genocide, Tasian murdered most of Laurencia's family. Sitting in prison, Tasian was overwhelmed with remorse. She wrote Laurencia and asked for forgiveness. Not only did Laurencia forgive her, she never once called Tasian a killer. Tasian says that Laurencia is the one who truly gave her freedom. Now that Tasian is out of prison, the women watch each other's children.

It took more than an apology and a couple letters to bridge what divided these women. Mbyo was established as a reconciliation village where the residents made a commitment to rebuild their lives after the war. The women attended group discussions on conflict resolution, committed to look after livestock and crops together, and shared a common bank to pay for health insurance.[16] The key was that the women focused on a common problem—rebuilding their lives after the war. If Hutus and Tutsis can learn to not only coexist but care for one another and invest in building a better future, we all can. Despite the artificial ethnic differences imposed on them, they demonstrated CQ Drive in their motivation to bridge their differences and used CQ Action to build a better future together.

Building a more just, equitable world for all ethnicities and races takes more than changing your profile picture or putting up a yard sign that says, "Stop Asian Hate." It means taking action to allow economic opportunity for everyone. Ideally, this includes pulling together a multiracial group of friends and colleagues to do things like:

+ Support businesses (restaurants, banks, shops, builders, landscape services, attorneys, etc.) owned by underrepresented groups.
+ Hold businesses and nonprofits accountable. What's being done at your dentist's office, religious community, golf club, and beyond to hire people of color at all levels, not just frontline service roles?
+ Petition your local school or university to hire administrators and staff from diverse backgrounds, to support underrepresented families and students, and to ensure curriculum includes a diversity of voices.
+ Disrupt racist systems, policies, and practices at work. This might include challenging a biased hiring policy or encouraging your employer to develop a supplier diversity program.
+ Vote for politicians who will support legislation that promotes more equitable opportunities and protections for all people.

What about the polarizing views surrounding whether race should be considered when recruiting a new staff member? Use a problem-solving approach to handle this as well. Get the hiring team to zoom out to an objective everyone can agree on, such as ensuring you find the best person for the job. Then use the diversity on your team to develop and evaluate criteria for the ideal candidate. This is tricky. It's not helpful to ask an African American colleague, "What will Black people think about this job posting?" But we need to ask the team to look at the posting through the lens of different groups. If only white people apply for the position, there's a problem. Why aren't any people of color interested in this kind of role? If only white people are interviewed, why are the only applicants who match the criteria white?

There are many excellent resources on how to manage bias in the hiring process, but my point is, this kind of solution-oriented approach moves us beyond polarizing, racialized rhetoric that stymies effectiveness. Culturally intelligent problem-solving not only maximizes the rich perspectives that come from a racially diverse group, it also helps bridge racial inequities.

Am I Exploiting Racism?

To be honest, I was leery of writing this chapter. If Fiji filmmaker Luke Thompson's adjacency with racial minorities is in question, mine most definitely is. My understanding of racial discrimination is mostly theoretical. Yet I can't write a book about our digital, diverse world without addressing one of the most polarizing issues facing us. Nor is it fair to put the burden of working toward racial equity solely on the oppressed.

It's not my place to be the primary voice for how to understand racism. But neither can I abdicate responsibility just because some might question my motives and criticize my attempts. I'd rather err on the side of being an ally and using my work to expose injustice than retreat and remain silent. I might be wrong. I often am. And I'm always open to how my well-intended attempts are not the best way to go about it, so I hope to keep learning from those with lived experience. In the words of one of the residents in Mbyo, Rwanda: "It is us—the people—who were most deeply affected by the genocide, so *it must also be us who change things for the better*."[17]

NINE

Pronouns

I first heard Rob Bell speak at the church he started in Grand Rapids, Michigan. My wife, Linda, and I were driving through on the way home to Chicago, and we were intrigued to experience the phenomenon of Rob Bell. He was a big deal in the world of evangelicalism at the time—a young, hip pastor who had started a church in a dilapidated shopping mall that grew to over ten thousand people almost overnight. You could spot people from his church all over town with their black-and-white "Love wins" bumper stickers.

The morning we visited, Rob was standing on stage in the middle of a former department store with the congregation sitting in the round. His teaching was about Hooters, a restaurant brand focused on female servers with tight-fitting T-shirts and short shorts. Rob never mentioned Hooters, but he sat in an orange restaurant booth and said something like, "Imagine a world where an entire business, started and run by men, is built around hiring young women to serve wings and beer but sex appeal is the primary thing on the menu.... This is the same world where women stand in line at the grocery store and see perfectly airbrushed models promising them the body of a lifetime. It's a world where men pay women a fraction of what they make to do the same job."

Rob continued for forty-five minutes. At one point I looked over and saw tears in Linda's eyes. When we left, she said, "Most of my life, the church taught me that I was the weaker sex, created to serve men. It's so empowering to hear a preacher acknowledge the objectification of women and see me for my whole humanity." The emphasis of Rob's teaching wasn't about the women wearing tight T-shirts. And it really wasn't about the men who sneak a drink at Hooters. It was about living in a world made by and for men.

Gender differences are polarizing because if you're anything other than a man in this world, you're automatically part of a marginalized group. More than half the world are women, yet when you look at heads of state, governments, and corporations, you almost always see men. Even the best of us men can't know what it's like to be treated as a minority, simply because of your anatomy. Gender inequality exists in every corner of the world. But cultural intelligence gives us the tools to address the inequities between he, she, they, and everyone.

The Power of Gender

It's hard to think of a more salient part of our identity than our gender. It's the first thing we notice about someone. Landscapers show up at our house and ask Linda if I'm around. But Linda oversees all of our house-related projects. A friend says his wife will call Linda to find a time when we can all get together. But I manage our social calendar. Trans women are told they can't compete on the women's team because they have biological advantages. But there's no consistent evidence trans women have an athletic edge.[1]

One Indian woman told me she grew up believing that a man raping his wife was acceptable, but consensual sex between any two unmarried individuals was abhorrent. Marriages, the modern workplace, and even cars are designed with men in mind. On average, women sit farther forward when driving a car than men do in order to see over the dashboard. But car seats are designed for a man's body, which puts women at greater risk of injury any time they get behind the wheel.[2] Our figured worlds teach us how to play our gender. There's no question there are real biological differences that separate males, females, intersex, and trans individuals. But it's the artificial differences scripted by our gendered worlds that create the most polarization and inequality. Let's start with a few foundational concepts.

Body Parts versus Identity

"Facts don't care about feelings! You're either a man or a woman. Just look at your anatomy." Some of the confusion surrounding gender identity stems from the ways that gender, sex, and sexuality are used interchangeably. To understand the power of gender, it's important to be clear about the differences in these core concepts.

Sex: Body parts. In school, we learned that XX chromosomes mean you're female; XY chromosomes mean you're male. That's an oversimplification, but let's start with that. Our sex is announced at birth when the doctor examines our body parts and says, "It's a boy!" When people argue against someone being transgender, they're using a biological argument: "You either have a vagina or you don't." They confuse sex with gender. When referring to the sex assigned at birth, the generally accepted nomenclature is "male" or "female."

Gender: Mind. Gender is how we think and behave within a range of possibilities between masculine and feminine. Most of us identify with the gender that fits our anatomy, but that too is an oversimplification. Masculinity among many twenty-somethings looks different than it did for their fathers. French philosopher Simone de Beauvoir said: "One is not born, but rather, becomes a woman." She argued that being a woman is not a natural fact; it's the cultural interpretation of our biology.[3] Gender is the costume we put on everyday based on the cultural scripts we're given. "Man" and "woman" are the terms used to refer to gender.

Sexuality: Attraction. A lot of debate surrounds whether sexuality is a biological orientation or a choice. For many years homosexuality was described as an orientation, to avoid attempts at reforming someone into being heterosexual. Yet a growing number of LGBTQ+ advocates say there's a fine line between calling homosexuality an orientation and acting as if it's an unfortunate genetic aberration that no one would ever choose. One lesbian writer says, "Some in the gay community wish to pass the buck for their choice of sexual identity to a rogue gene." She's concerned that calling homosexuality an orientation mocks those who have proudly chosen to be gay, as if they need to be trained out of it.[4]

Sex, gender, and attraction work interdependently with nature and experience both playing a role. But how do we develop such strong ideas about how to play our gender?

Where We Get Our Gender Scripts

A couple years after Linda and I first heard Rob Bell speak, we moved to Grand Rapids and began attending his church. It was a place where he challenged people to think about creating a different world than the one made up of Hooters, airbrushed models, and homophobia. Bell's book, *Love Wins*, landed him on national television shows and on *Time* magazine's top one hundred most influential people. His driving purpose was bringing people together to bring measurable change to the world. The differences in gender, race, politics, or nationality weren't the focus. Instead, it was to serve together to support microenterprise development, access to clean water, or opportunities to mentor kids in underresourced communities. But how did Rob develop his views about gender?

My Mother Taught Me...

The number-one way most of us learn how to play our gender is from our parents. We watch their activities and subconsciously learn the rules and structures for how to behave. Who should fix the leaky faucet? Who should make dinner? Who controls the money? Who decides whether we're having sex?

Rob grew up in a conservative Christian home, and his dad was a federal judge appointed by President Reagan. How did he go from that environment to being such an advocate for gender equality? His family was filled with strong women. His grandmother in the Midwest had her own television show, and his other grandma was an art teacher in Los Angeles. "My dad held my mom is such high esteem," Rob said. "She got a master's degree from UCLA when she was twenty-one and my dad was in awe of how capable and intelligent, she was. Our dinner table was a talking free-for-all. It was assumed everybody had something interesting to say. And my sister was and is a force of nature—so creative and dynamic from a young age." What Rob saw modeled early on was: "Everybody has their path and a particular gift to give; their gender shouldn't stand in the way of that."[5]

Yet research indicates that gender modeling at home still defaults to traditional norms, even in progressive cultures and families. Women in the US do 67 percent more household chores than men. Parents encourage relationships with families and kids who model similar behaviors and values. In return, peers reinforce the values parents teach, with school, workplaces, faith communities, and the media further reinforcing or challenging the gendered scripts our parents model.[6]

Hollywood's Dirty Little Secret

Rob decided he no longer fit as a pastor of a megachurch and moved to Los Angeles, where there would be a broader audience for his message. A few months after moving, he told me: "Hollywood is the most conservative place I've ever been." *Really? You were a pastor in the Midwest and your dad was a Republican-appointed judge.* But Rob was serious. He found Hollywood to be unusually averse to taking risks, where the good old boys made money exploiting overused stereotypes. He said, "I remember my first conference call with a group of network executives and they were asking the strangest questions. They had no desire to make something new or stretch people. It was like they were all just trying to keep their jobs and not take any risks. They were in a malaise."

Numerous studies support Rob's claim. The virtual reality created by Hollywood is one predominantly shaped by risk-averse white men who perpetuate a skewed, unequal world on and off the screen. For every eight films directed by men, one is directed by a woman.[7] Women speak only 30 percent as much as men in top-grossing movies, and a significantly smaller percentage are in lead roles. Women of color are almost nonexistent in lead roles. In fact, you're more likely to see an alien or sci-fi creature speaking on screen than an Asian or Latina woman.[8] Hollywood creates worlds run by and for men.

Last summer, my daughter Grace roped me into watching a couple episodes of *Selling Sunset*, a scripted reality TV show based on the luxury real-estate market in Los Angeles. The cast is the Oppenheim Group, a real-estate brokerage run by bachelor twins and staffed by a group of competitive, glamorous women who show houses while wearing stilettos. Watching the male bosses bark orders and seeing the women use their sex appeal to sell houses made me think, *How is this any different than Hooters?* But the dominant theme of *Selling Sunset* isn't as much the sex appeal as it is the bickering between women. In one episode Christine says: "My definition of loyalty is, if I want to bury a bitch, you'll be there with a shovel." There's no evidence women gossip any more than men. But Hollywood directors like Adam DiVello, creator of *Selling Sunset* and a list of similar reality shows, keep these tired stereotypes alive. Without even realizing it, we willingly lap it up.[9]

Feminist Theories versus Frat Parties

I went to a private Christian college. Although college exposed me to broader views of gender than I had growing up at home, my professors critiqued feminism and similar progressive ideas. In contrast, my daughters attended large secular universities. I don't think a semester went by that they weren't assigned a reading on feminist thought. They were repeatedly exposed to progressive ideas about gender and sexuality. Universities were the first to normalize sharing your pronouns, they require sexual harassment training for faculty and students, and they have policies that require inclusive language on syllabi, papers, and so forth.

But there's an aspect present in many universities that is far more patriarchal than anything I experienced at my small Christian college. When my daughter first started explaining the norms of frat parties to me—girls get in "free," but boys have to pay—I was incensed. "So, your body is a commodity that gets you free beer?" I had reason to be alarmed. Emily attended University of Southern California, where the Kappa Sigma fraternity publishes a gullet report that tracks which sorority girls "put out." Their internal document reads: "I want raw data on who fucks and who doesn't." At North Carolina State's Pi Kappa Phi chapter the pledge book includes lines such as "It will be short and painful, just like when I rape you." And a fraternity at University of Richmond sent out a party invitation that said: "Tonight's the type of night that makes fathers afraid to send their daughters away to school."[10]

How does this happen at the same institutions leading the way in feminist thought and sponsoring events on women's empowerment? Journalist Alexandra Robbins went inside fraternities to get an up-close look. Students who are part of fraternities and sororities are more likely to cling to crass gender stereotypes than other students are. Many universities have cracked down on the hazing, sex, and alcohol that goes on in Greek life. Rollins points to numerous strengths that come from fraternities and sororities, something I observed firsthand through my daughter's participation.[11] But hegemonic gender modeling occurs in some of the most unlikely places. The impact on the gender scripts we play is powerful. The question is whether we accept it or rewrite it.

Through the Eyes of Gender

Let's expand our CQ Knowledge by looking at a few examples of how our gendered worlds polarize the way we think and behave. How about the controversial subject of women's head coverings? While many progressives view head coverings as oppressive and restrictive, many Muslim women find enormous freedom from wearing the hijab as an expression of their identity and faith. In Islam the hair is the crown of a woman's beauty, and many women prefer to reserve their beauty for their husbands and families alone. Some Islamic women have told me that making them go to the office without their hijab would be like telling a Western woman to wear a bikini to the office.

When men *force* women to cover their heads, it's oppressive because it's no longer a choice. Many Iranian women had been unveiled for years when the Ayatollah Khomeini made it illegal for them to be in public without the hijab. It's also oppressive to *ban* women from wearing a hijab as is done in some Western contexts. It comes down to giving women agency to dress in ways that express who they are. As my daughters became teenagers, I extolled the virtues of dressing modestly: "I know how men think and I don't want you sending the wrong message." They challenged my reasoning: "You're giving men the power to dictate how we dress." Whether its burqas or bikinis, women should have the agency to dress themselves.

What about the gendered scripts given to men? Boys experience more reproach for deviating from gender norms and more reward for following them. If you "act masculine" and excel in male-dominated careers, you'll make more money and have more power. But you pay a price if you abandon the script for masculinity. Many parents are excited when their little girl wants a toolkit but are nervous when their son wants to sew.[12] Masculinity scripts have shifted a lot over the past couple decades. Men in some contexts are just as likely to do yoga as hunt. Men have become more comfortable unmasking their emotions and staying home to be the primary caregiver.[13] But these shifts are largely limited to a subset of upwardly mobile individuals, typically living in Western, cosmopolitan communities. Even there, dominant scripts about masculinity loom large.

Actor Justin Baldoni gave a fascinating TED Talk about how playing macho men on screen shaped the way he plays the script of being a man in real life. Baldoni didn't grow up with a lot of the traditional gender stereotypes, but his life on screen has been playing characters who ooze machismo, charisma, and power. Do an Internet search for his name and you retrieve countless images of his ripped, shirtless body as a male escort or a naughty heartthrob. Playing these kinds of roles repeatedly made Baldoni more conscious of the gender script he wants to play in real life. The dominant expectations of US men are: the drive to win at all costs, desiring multiple sexual partners, suppressing emotions, risky behavior, physical aggression, dominance, independence, work as a life priority, power over women, heterosexual, and status[14] Baldoni started turning down roles that perpetuated these macho stereotypes because he realized these scripts were shaping his performance in real life.[15] Even men benefit from transcending a male-centered world with dogmatic scripts about how to behave.

What about the large population of trans individuals? As a freshman athlete on the boys' track team at a Connecticut high school, Terry Miller held his own, but he failed to qualify for any postseason events. That changed when Miller came out as a trans girl in her sophomore year. Miller started running against girls and won five state championships and two New England titles. Miller's success continued through high school. The girls who lost to Miller argued that they were at a disadvantage because Miller still had the genetics of a young man. Local parents and coaches started online petitions to require a testosterone suppression requirement for trans girls.[16]

The debates surrounding trans athletes are intense, and they should be. Women have been fighting for decades to have equal opportunity in sports; some women have found the most unlikely allies in conservatives who are defending women's rights to have fair, equitable competition. Trans athletes say they're simply asking to be included, putting many liberals in the uncomfortable position of choosing trans rights or women's rights. There are no coherent guidelines across national, much less international athletic communities. And the science is limited at best. Some evidence suggests that men who undergo testosterone suppression for a year have body strength on par with their cisgender peers, while other research shows that men who transitioned retained most of the strength and muscle mass they had before the treatment.[17] Groups like the International Olympic Committee (IOC) are faced with two irreconcilable positions—determining eligibility based on one's declared gender or with a biological litmus test.

None of these either/or polarities work. The IOC, governments, and athletic associations may want to study the Special Olympics' approach, where they address issues of competitive fairness among disabled athletes by creating more categories. Sex, like gender, exists on a spectrum so all athletes may be better served by additional categories that make twenty-first-century athletics fair, inclusive, and safe. I don't pretend to know the best workable solution to these issues. I just know that we're pitting would-be allies against each other and turning these differences into another "us versus them" culture war. We need solutions that create fair competition in sports, include everyone, and don't undermine the progress women have made over the past fifty years. A trans person's experience doesn't lessen my experience or identity. There's room on the field for all of us. We must create space to listen to one another and use our collective brain power to come up with solutions that honor each person's humanity and allow us to effectively solve problems big and small together.

CQ Solutions

The forces scripting our gendered behavior are everywhere, and the pressure to conform is seductive. But there are ways cultural intelligence can help us rewrite our scripts, build a more equitable world, and work together to address issues we all care about.

CQ Drive provides the motivation to remember that work teams with gender diversity consistently perform better in sales, profits, and productivity than male-dominated teams do.[18] CQ Knowledge helps us understand that language like "hey guys," "welcome ladies and gentlemen," and "mankind," excludes large groups of people. If you don't believe me, try replacing "hey guys" with "hey ladies" to a coed group and see how the men respond. CQ Strategy puts us on alert for gender inequity. For example, the next time you see a long line outside the women's bathroom, stop and think about why architects continue to design buildings with equal size bathrooms, despite the different needs of men and women. And if a large office complex only has one gender-neutral bathroom, think about how that affects your trans colleagues every day. CQ Action equips us to use language that may feel foreign or wrong to us as an attempt to avoid unnecessarily alienating our friends and colleagues (e.g., use of "they" if that is what a trans individual prefers).

But let's go deeper. How can we use cultural intelligence to work together across gender divides to address common problems?

You Can Go Your Own Way

Cultural intelligence begins with taking responsibility for the way we play our own gender. Although we have no voice in the gender script we're given when we enter the world, we do as we mature. Like Justin Baldoni, we have agency to determine how to rewrite our scripts.

Anthropologist Debra Skinner interviewed women in Nepal to understand the intersections of caste and gender. She conducted interviews on the second story of the home where she was staying. When Debra went to the door to greet Gyanumaya, her next interviewee, she couldn't find her. Gyanumaya was already upstairs. She had scaled the wall of the house and entered through the second-level balcony to avoid the taboo of walking through the kitchen of a higher-status woman. There was no script that told Gyanumaya what to do in this situation. It's not like she made it a practice of scaling walls to enter buildings, but she improvised on the spot based on her interpretation in the moment.

On the one hand, this speaks to how powerfully the scripts about caste and gender play. But in a strange way, I find hope in what Gyanumaya did because it shows the agency we have to make decisions on our own when the script isn't clear. If that agency can be supported and further developed, women like Gyanumaya can begin to rewrite the dehumanizing parts of the scripts they've been handed. Exercising agency for ourselves and others is one of the most powerful solutions for addressing gender inequality.[19] We lose nothing by agreeing to refer to a colleague as "they" even if we don't understand their preference. And as we begin to work together to address problems we both care about, we quickly see that my opinion about how you play your gender is largely irrelevant.

Be an Ally

Another key strategy is to use the power of allyship to solve problems together. One time I was in a meeting with Christy, a vice president at the university where we both worked. Christy was one of the most vocal women on campus advocating the importance of equal opportunities for women faculty, staff, and students. The guy chairing our meeting tried to provoke Christy. I was waiting for Christy to confront him, but she didn't. She engaged in the meeting in light of her responsibilities and said nothing about the pats on her shoulder, the soccer mom jokes, and the chides that she probably didn't get the sports analogies. As we left the meeting, I said, "Christy! I can't believe you took that!" She said, "Yeah, I was hoping you would say something."

Everyone expects women like Christy to speak up for women. But it would have meant much more if I had done so. It's not that Christy needed me to speak *for her*. It's that gender equality can't just be a women's issue. I care about equality for women, and my male counterpart needed to know that *I* found his banter inappropriate. Most men say they support gender equality, but they believe women are treated equally. One study found that 77 percent of men didn't see harassment as a problem in their organizations; yet 38 percent of their female peers reported a recent form of sexual harassment.

British author Caroline Criado Perez says: "Even the best of men can't know what it's like to go through the world as a person with a body which some other people treat as an access-all-areas amusement arcade."[20] But I sure as hell am determined to understand what it's like. Here are some ways I'm trying to be a better ally:

+ Listen, listen, listen. And when I think it's time to speak, I try to listen more, and some more after that. This is a practical way to use CQ Action.
+ Use CQ Knowledge to recognize the varied experiences and preferences among women. Trans women of color have different needs than cisgender women. Women without children have different needs than mothers.
+ I've joined a growing number of men who have decided to turn down speaking at conferences with only male speakers or panels. Or I recommend a woman for a high-profile speaking invitation, preferably to address something other than "women's issues." If you are a man, when the boss asks you to lead a big project, recommend a female or trans colleague to take the lead and agree to be a supportive team member.
+ Volunteer for tasks often assigned to women such as taking minutes, scheduling meetings, or ordering lunch. Differences in how much time men and women spend on non-promotable tasks are one reason women are promoted less quickly than their male counterparts are.
+ Notice sexist jokes and comments. See who is included in decision-making and information-sharing. Ask women about

their experiences. And unlike what I did in that meeting with Christy, speak up—not because women and trans people can't speak for themselves; but because we all need to promote equality and respect for everyone.[21]

Address Real Problems

A couple years ago, I was talking with a group of women at a Fortune 500 company who were frustrated with the agenda the company put together for International Women's Day. The day began with a women's-only yoga session followed by brunch. At mid-day, Facebook's Cheryl Sandberg was giving a talk on balancing work and family life. Mid-afternoon, a select group of women would have tea with the guys in the C-suite. And the day ended with fruity cocktails at the restaurant across the street. One woman was waving the agenda in her hand and said, "Do they really think *this* is what we want?" As the women discussed it, one guy chimed in: "Hang on a second. Are you saying we shouldn't recognize women's day? Weren't gals involved in putting the agenda together?" The women looked at each other, rolled their eyes, and explained that they were looking for meaningful initiatives by the company that truly addressed gender inequities, rather than trivial, albeit well-intended, activities.

This doesn't feel all that different from Bic's misfire when they created "Bic for Her" pens—special pens for women that come in pink and purple and are especially suited to fit a woman's hand. If you want a good laugh, read some of the Amazon reviews where women sarcastically ask, "Do you have any special pens for 'that time of the month'?" And "If I write something with these pens, does that mean whatever I write is still wrong?"

Treating everyone the same isn't the answer. But pink pens and brunch don't address inequity. A better approach to International Women's Day would be presentations on how the company is ensuring more women are hired into leadership positions, how to confront mansplaining without losing your job, and workshops for men on how to be an ally. As one woman said: "Just pay me equally and I'll buy my own damn brunch."

Women have always worked. For many years and in many places, they have worked unpaid and invisibly, but they have *always* worked. However, the modern workplace was designed and created by and for men. The location, work hours, regulatory standards were all designed around men's lives. Women's work is not some add-on to give meaning before and after giving birth. Indra Nooyi, former CEO of PepsiCo, says that what women need is for companies to make wholesale changes. The career clock and biological clock are in direct conflict for women. Women move into middle management just about the time they must take time off to give birth. Women like Nooyi want everyone working together to create structures and systems that accommodate the issues uniquely faced by women.

Something Has to Change

In 2004, Thangjam Manorama was raped and murdered by members of the Indian army. Five days later, thirty local women marched through the streets naked carrying a board that said: "The Indian Army raped us." The protest led to the government launching an investigation on the case and creating policies to promote the protection of women. Similar protests and campaigns are changing what happens behind closed doors in board rooms, bedrooms, and frat houses across the world. Things are improving. Gender equality is increasing in almost every country in the world. But the World Economic Forum projects it will take another century for governments and organizations to close the gender gap.[22]

We can't wait a hundred years, and we don't have to. We need to take things into our own hands. Allyship, systemic change, and working together to address common problems have the power to bridge gender inequity. And together, we can build a more culturally intelligent world where everyone can thrive, regardless of their pronouns. But what if doing so goes against your religion?

TEN

G/god/s

Jose and Soo-Jin are a power couple. They met at Columbia as undergraduates and fell hard for each other. Soo-Jin completed her MBA by the time she was twenty-three, and she was vice president at a Fortune 500 company by thirty. Jose is a cardiologist who was recruited by several top hospitals across the US. A year ago, they both accepted lucrative job offers in Mexico City, where they moved with their two kids. Soo-Jin is a second-generation Korean American, and Jose is a third-generation Mexican American. It took a while for Soo-Jin's parents to get used to the idea of their daughter marrying a non-Korean, but that paled in contrast to the idea of her marrying an atheist.

Soo-Jin grew up in a Christian family. Her dad is a presbyterian minister, and Soo-Jin remained actively involved in church throughout her studies. Growing up, she repeatedly heard her dad quote the Apostle Paul: "Do not be unequally yoked," a Bible verse used to instill the dangers of marrying outside the faith. When Soo-Jin started dating Jose, she was haunted by her dad's words from when she was young: "My greatest fear is you end up marrying someone who doesn't love Jesus. That would break my heart."

Jose grew up nominally Catholic. His grandmother went to mass every Sunday, but his mother thought it was ridiculous that a woman couldn't be a priest. Today, Jose is an atheist. He thinks it's fine if other people believe in God, but his confidence rests in hard work, logic, and science. Soo-Jin still identifies as a Christian, but the neat categories of faith she grew up with don't work very well for her anymore. Her parents are worried that she still hasn't found a church in Mexico City, and they're deeply concerned about their grandchildren. Every week they send Soo-Jin a link to watch their church service online.

For some, issues of faith are little more than esoteric, existential considerations. For others, they strike at the core of who to marry, how to vote, and whether to attend a gay wedding. This is a very personal chapter for me. Although my faith has evolved a great deal in fifty years, it remains an important part of my identity. Religious divisions are behind wars, abuse, and broken families. Yet the transcendence and higher consciousness associated with faith might be a critical pathway out of polarization. People of faith can readily find common causes they care about, but it takes cultural intelligence to address them together.

The Power of Religion

People choose careers, move to the other side of the world, and give away large sums of money all because of their faith. Massive institutions are organized around faith, some with multi-billion-dollar budgets. There are more Methodist churches in the US than post offices and more places of worship in India than all the schools and colleges combined. Faith permeates life in most of the world. Even in Europe, often viewed as an outlier among the faithful, the majority say they believe in God.[1]

One of the ways we cope with the mysteries of the natural world is through belief in otherworldly powers. This is true across every culture in the world. Jose isn't as purely rational as he says he is. Shortly before he and Soo-Jin moved to Mexico, he said, "I don't want to jinx things, but this move is coming together perfectly." Why does a rationally minded atheist need to insert a caution about jinxing something? Is he really concerned he might undo the great plan he's put together by talking about it? Even if you're short on faith, you've probably begged your car to start—*please, please, please*—or complained that your computer is cursed and has a mind of its own. Are these merely idioms? Maybe. But it's more likely that all of us have some tendency to detect an otherworldly effect when a situation is beyond our control.

Whether someone dismisses the afterlife as crazy talk or dogmatically affirms that their loved ones are in heaven, both actions require a leap of faith. The truth is, none of us know what happens after we die because none of us have died and lived to tell about it. We need to approach conversations of faith and the figured worlds of religion with humility, curiosity, and openness. An honest look at faith begins with using CQ Knowledge to understand the strong links between place and what we believe. Most of us would probably believe differently if we grew up in a different part of the world. Religious scholar J. H. McKenna describes a party where the host tried guessing everyone's religion. To a woman from Arkansas, the host said, "Let me guess. You're Southern Baptist." He was right. Next up, he asked Edwin where he's from.

Edwin: Minneapolis

Host: Lutheran?

Edwin: That's crazy! Yes!

Rebecca: Kanab, Utah

Host: Are you Mormon?

Rebecca: That's outrageous! Are you psychic or something?

Asif: Quetta, Pakistan

Host: Muslim

Asif: This is too weird. Yes.

Lupe: Arequipa, Peru

Host: Catholic

Lupe: Yes! It's almost scary!

Shakuntila: I'm from Mumbai, India.

Host: Would you happen to be Hindu?

Shakuntila: Most excellent! You are indeed a psychic!

The host did this with more than twenty guests, and most of his guesses were right, including that Ditte from Viborg, Denmark, was an atheist.[2] There's a strong correlation between where you grew up and your faith. Of course, there are exceptions. I've met Christians in Indonesia, Japan, and Somalia, and Muslims in Australia, Venezuela, and Germany. But most of these individuals grew up in those faiths. Fewer than 1 percent of adults switch religions.[3]

Soo-Jin's grandparents converted to Christianity after they emigrated to the US. Christians are 25 percent of the population in South Korea, but they're 75 percent of the Korean American population. There are a couple reasons why. First, most Korean immigrants are middle class, and middle-class Koreans are more likely to be Christian. Second, Korean immigrants learn that the best way to meet other Koreans in the US is at church. One Korean woman said, "I never went to church back in Korea, nor was I a believer, but I began to attend shortly after my arrival here... I went to church to see other Koreans...to talk to them, to hang around with them."[4]

Our families are the biggest influence on what we believe.[5] My mom and her siblings grew up following my grandfather's ministry across Canada. He started a seminary, planted numerous churches, and led the largest Evangelical denomination in the country. All five kids in my mom's family were devout Christians except my Uncle John. I remember our family praying fervently for him to be converted, but it never happened. There's an interesting mystery about who accepts the family religion and who doesn't. Most adults pass along their childhood faith to their kids. This is something that has surprised me in watching my own peers. Many of the individuals who seemed the least engaged in the faith as adolescents are some of the most strident believers as middle-aged adults.

If you're part of a family where faith is central, there's a great deal of pressure to espouse belief, even if you don't. A Qatari friend told me he dismissed the tenets of Islam long ago but to renounce his faith would result in incredible loneliness. He would no longer be invited to iftar, he would have missed out on the momentous pilgrimage to Hajj with his father and brothers, and he may not even be able to live on the family compound any longer. Little does his family know that he's part of a Facebook group for Muslims who have left the faith. For many people, there's a high price to pay for abandoning the faith of your figured world.

Through the Eyes of Faith

Religion and culture are two sides of the same coin—whether it's the way Hinduism shapes life across India or the prevalence of the European Enlightenment on Protestant theology. Yet there are enormous differences among people of the same faith from different cultures. Understanding this was the first step in broadening my worldview and building my CQ Knowledge. The different ways Coptic Christians in Ethiopia, Pentecostals in Brazil, Anglicans in Singapore, and Evangelicals in North America understand and apply the Bible were mind-boggling.

One of Soo-Jin's favorite Bible stories is the Prodigal Son—the story Jesus tells of a young son who asks for his inheritance early. The prodigal takes the money, spends it wildly, and ends up destitute in a pig pen. One study asked Evangelical pastors, "Why did the prodigal end up in the pig pen?"

> Russian pastors said: "It was because there was a famine in the land."
>
> Tanzanian pastors said: "It was because no one gave him anything to eat."
>
> American pastors said: "It was because he squandered the money he inherited."[6]

If you look at what the Bible story actually says, all three interpretations are there. But the way we read and understand the sacred texts of our faiths is strongly influenced by our cultural backgrounds.

Diverse expressions of faith and understandings of Scripture are a treasure trove to be mined by people of faith. But this raises some uncomfortable questions about whose interpretation is right and which truths are transcendent versus those that are simply cultural constructions. Rather than being afraid of those differences, cultural intelligence allows us to zoom in on them and acknowledge the way our cultural backgrounds inform the way we read sacred texts. For me, there are interpretations that are too far adrift from what the original text says. I can't just conclude: "The prodigal ended up in the pig pen because he liked farming." But when you combine the US emphasis of responsibility, the Tanzanian emphasis on community, and the Russian emphasis on circumstances, you have a much more well-rounded interpretation of this ancient story. Your perspective doesn't discount mine and vice versa. Instead, this expansion of our CQ Knowledge takes our understanding deeper.

I used to say there's less diversity across Islam than Christianity because of the limited priority given to translating the Koran. But that's not true. Indonesian Muslims use a uniquely Javanese approach to cleansing before Ramadan, cannons are shot in Lebanon to trigger the start of iftar, and Emirati kids roam their neighborhoods in bright clothing before Ramadan to collect sweets and nuts. Diversity abounds in how Muslims practice their faith too.

The more awkward question is how one young person's commitment to faith becomes a suicide mission while another's results in a lifetime of service. As a first-generation immigrant in the US from Egypt, comedian Ramy Youssef initially downplayed his faith for fear of being villainized. It was clear that people thought Muslims were the bad guys. While Ramy couldn't deny the reality of honor killings done in the name of Islam or his discomfort that Saudi Arabia didn't allow women to drive, he knew these didn't really have anything to do with what the Koran teaches. In *Ramy*, his semiautographical Hulu series, the main character takes what he calls an "allah carte" approach to Islam. He doesn't drink but he has premarital sex. Other Muslims on the show drink but won't date anyone outside the faith. In making sense of his own faith, Ramy says, "Everyone has a code, and I think that transcends any specific culture or faith."[7] This isn't unique to Islam. We have a way of picking and choosing which parts of our faith suit us.

It used to be that marrying outside your faith was unheard of. Today it's much more common. One study found that 40 percent of Americans who married since 2010 have a spouse from a different faith. Many marriages are like Jose and Soo-Jin's, where one partner is religiously affiliated and the other is a "none."[8] "Nones" are the fastest growing religious group in North America and Europe—individuals who identify with no religion. More than 20 percent of the US population and 90 percent of Europeans are "nones." They still believe in God, but they reject the institution of religion.

Soo-Jin always assumed she would marry a Christian, but Jose demonstrated the values most important to her—compassion, purpose-filled work, generosity, and integrity. To her, whether he was Muslim, Christian, or agnostic was insignificant. She admits, however, that ending up with an atheist may be even harder for her family to accept than if he was a devout Jew. I asked Jose if there was a point in time when he became an atheist. "I think I've always been an atheist," he said. "But it took a long time before I felt comfortable with the label." He was skeptical when his grandma buried a Virgin Mary in her front yard for good luck and when his mom thanked God for answering their prayers and diverting a hurricane to the west. *Did the people to the west just not pray hard enough?* But it was the Catholic Church's position on women, homosexuality, and abortion that convinced Jose he couldn't be part of an institution he believed was doing more harm than good. With time, he concluded he didn't see evidence for a so-called God. Despite this, many of the people

Jose admires most are people of faith, including Martin Luther King Jr., Mother Theresa, Nelson Mandela, and of course Soo-Jin.

Although family strongly shapes our religious beliefs, we have agency. We can choose to accept the faith we're given, modify how and what we believe, or walk away entirely. But it's never as easy as all of that. The angst Soo-Jin feels about wanting her parents' approval, even as an adult, is shared by many across the world. Polarization often stems from the fear of being kicked out of your community. Soo-Jin is faced with reconciling many conflicting figured worlds. How do we tap the reverence, compassion, and altruism of faith to bridge religious divides rather than making them worse? And how do we use the power of cultural intelligence to address common problems across the figured worlds of faith?

CQ Solutions

Let's look at how the CQ competencies help bridge worlds divided by faith. CQ Drive gives us an openness and curiosity to respectfully consider different religious perspectives rather than beginning with an impulse to prove them wrong. CQ Knowledge helps us go beyond biased indoctrinations about other faiths by providing a more objective understanding of the differences. CQ Strategy helps us plan in light of religious differences. For example, you can use CQ Strategy to plan a social gathering by being mindful of a group's dietary preferences or restrictions. And CQ Action gives us the flexibility to adapt to the religious customs and beliefs of our friends and colleagues without feeling like we somehow have to compromise our own convictions and beliefs.

Let's zoom in on specific ways cultural intelligence can help us solve common problems that transcend our religious differences.

Be Curious

The one trait that consistently predicts cultural intelligence is *openness*—a curiosity about the world and an eagerness to learn new things, or CQ

Drive. I know many people who are open to different foods or cultural traditions, but their CQ Drive stops when it comes to religion. This can be just as true of atheists. Writer Thane Rosenbaum says, "Atheism can become as nasty, hostile and ill-informed as the religious fanatics they so thoroughly condemn."[9]

The journey toward cultural intelligence begins with seeing the beauty in many different quests to understand the transcendent. I used to be unnerved hearing the Muslim call to prayer. It was unfamiliar and if I'm honest, it made me feel a bit unsafe. I was less triggered seeing a Chinese shopkeeper burn incense for Buddha, but that still seemed alien to me. I had a similar sense of otherness when listening to an agnostic professor rant about religion as the source of all evil in the world.

Today I'm intrigued by any response to the transcendent. That didn't happen quickly. However, as I began to interact with more individuals who held different beliefs, rather than just reading summaries shared with me from Christian apologetics or newsclips, Muslims, Buddhists, and Sikhs seemed less foreign to me. I remember sitting with a group of Saudi airline pilots smoking a sheesha pipe and they asked if I was a Christian. I didn't know if this was a setup, but I acknowledged I was raised Christian. Their faces lit up and one of them said, "We love to meet other believers!" We talked about our kids, the challenges of regularly traveling far from our families, and our shared value for integrity and generosity. These men didn't seem anything like the caricatures I had been taught.

Openness doesn't mean abandoning our beliefs. I'm not sure why so many are afraid to be open to others' beliefs. If our beliefs are true, won't that become more evident when we're exposed to other ways of explaining the mysteries of the world? Most interfaith advocates focus on celebrating the common themes of compassion, sacrifice, and service. But we gain more from using CQ Knowledge to study the *differences* between faiths. Study something you admire about another faith that isn't as core to yours. There's beauty in every tradition. All the major religions agree that something is wrong with the world, but they have vastly different conclusions about the source of the problem and how to address it. Buddhism teaches the power of enlightenment to address the problem of suffering. Judaism is focused on returning to God from exile, and Hinduism highlights devotion through meditation, release, and forgiveness.[10] There's so much existential truth and wonder to be discovered in each of these religions.

Jose finds it easier than Soo-Jin to approach her parents with a posture of openness. He sees beauty in their selfless devotion and dedicated service. He used to view them as less intelligent for believing in God, but over time he's come to appreciate and learn from their single-minded focus on God, their dedication to pray about everything, and their unconditional love. Jose's CQ Drive motivated him to understand what truly informed their dedication, loyalty, and compassion. Instead of coming into a weekend with them to debate their beliefs, Jose used his CQ Action to ask his father-in-law to describe the insights he gains from his daily practices of prayer, Bible study, and meditation. Instead of cringing when his mother-in-law describes any good thing as a "God-thing," Jose asks her how she thinks God was involved in making that thing happen. Taking a more open, curious approach not only helped frame Jose's own mind-set, it also began to motivate Soo-Jin to treat her parents' beliefs and values with the same kind of respect and curiosity she uses when encountering the beliefs and values of different cultures.

Form a Faith Club

After 9/11, Ranya Idliby, an American Muslim, asked two other mothers to write an interfaith children's book with her. Together they could highlight the connections between their three faiths—Judaism, Christianity, and Islam. The women were enthused about the project, but quickly discovered their own stereotypes and misunderstandings about one another. They committed to a journey of friendship and discovery, the highlights of which are chronicled in their memoir, *The Faith Club*.[11]

The women's conversations didn't lack conviction. They argued and listened. Too many interfaith gatherings include the same group of liberals sitting together, drafting documents about how all religious people should be dialoguing with each other. It's all about the conversation. The same things get repeated, convincing each other that it's vitally important with little impact on the rest of the world. The three women continued to meet and debate, constantly expanding their CQ Knowledge as they did so. With time, they admitted to their own prejudices and saw that it was *them*, more than their kids, who needed to know how to find each other through their different faith journeys. They questioned themselves and each other. That was part of what made it true connection. The women weren't there to proselytize each other, but neither were they there to simply "agree to disagree."

A few questions I use when talking to friends with different beliefs include:

+ What do most people get wrong about what you believe?
+ What about your religion makes you uncomfortable (e.g., its history, its position on various issues, its reputation, etc.)?
+ What doubts do you have?
+ What is your perception of my beliefs?

I used to shy away from talking about my faith publicly. In fact, a friend who read an early draft of this book was surprised I spoke so openly about my faith compared to watching me in other professional settings. Too many of us have been reluctant to talk about this critical part of our identities, particularly at work. A majority of Fortune 100 companies don't make a single reference to faith on their diversity landing pages, and only 5 percent have employee resource groups (ERGs) that relate to faith or belief.[12] Yet faith is such a foundational part of how the world operates and core to the driving motivations and identities for many people. Companies would do well to become more comfortable talking about religious diversity along with the other forms of identity more often addressed.

American Airlines CEO Doug Parker created a stir when he demonstrated CQ Action by joining his Muslim employees by fasting during Ramadan. Parker, himself a Christian, said that joining the Ramadan fast allowed him to empathize with his Muslim staff around the world who were fasting and praying and it allowed him to feel others' pain, suffering, loneliness, poverty, and hunger. Many Christian employees and customers were incensed that Parker didn't make the same kind of explicit recognition of Christian holidays and practices. But it's unlikely that the Christians of a Texas-based company feel alone and invisible when they celebrate Christmas and Easter. They're surrounded by supportive colleagues and company practices that are built around their religion's holidays.

It's hard to vilify Christians, Muslims, Hindus, or atheists when they become your friends and colleagues. Find a group of people with whom you have profound disagreements on the fundamental issues of life and work to understand each other. That kind of dialogue and relationship can lead to true change, which leads to the final and most important strategy for overcoming religious polarization.

On a Mission Together

The key driver behind terrorism and religious fundamentalism isn't Scriptural, it's sociological. Suicide bombers and religious zealots aren't putting the next interfaith dinner on their schedules. They're joining institutions, following leaders, and subscribing to online forums that give them a cause and a community. Leaders manipulate sacred texts to support their agendas, and build institutions to recruit, inspire, and train young people to act in destructive ways.[13] That same sociological power can be leveraged to promote compassion, understanding, and service.

The way out of a polarizing faith is the same way into it—communities that work together to build a different kind of world. Problem-solving has the supernatural power to bridge our differences.

Hadassah Ein Kerem Hospital in Jerusalem is in the middle of the Israeli–Palestinian conflict, a polarization that stems from differences of place, faith, and ethnicity, but religion is at the center of it all. The hospital is sitting on land that was home to an Arab village until the Israeli army attacked it. Outside the walls of the hospital, the sea of distrust and violence wages war. But inside, Jews, Muslims, and Christians work together to treat patients. Their focus is using their diverse skills to treat their fellow humanity regardless of ethnicity or religion. Dr. Chaim Lotan says, "I feel we have to find a solution—at the end of the day young people are killed for nothing, in the name of nothing." For him, part of the solution was recruiting a diverse team of technicians, doctors, and nurses from Jerusalem who transcend their religious differences by working together to care for their fellow citizens and keep them alive.[14]

Dr. Lotan says, "For me it doesn't matter who [a patient] is. Once they are here, they're our people." He has walked by bombings on the way to work and treated the attackers a few hours later. He hires Palestinian residents like Rashad Rizeq, a medical professional some patients will find easier to trust. The goal isn't diversity. It's to provide the best treatment possible to every patient regardless of their beliefs. Lotan defends and supports his staff who are sometimes mistreated by family and patients. The Israeli government, the Palestinian Authority, and the EU help pick up the tab for patients to be treated, regardless of their ethnicity or faith.[15] This is the kind of grassroots leadership and support needed to use our differences to create a better world for all of us.

Across the ocean, Eboo Patel developed the Interfaith Youth Core because he was frustrated that young people were absent from most US interfaith gatherings. He started by gathering youth from a variety of faiths to meet weekly to get to know each other and serve together. The youth had assignments, alternating between understanding and action.

One week each student had to present a faith hero from their tradition who exemplified a shared value like hospitality. The next week the students served homeless people together or tutored refugee children. Eventually Patel developed an interfaith residential community where youth live and serve together for a year.[16]

Most of us won't be joining an interfaith commune, nor am I suggesting we should give up assembling with our own congregations. But faith communities can live out their respective missions much more effectively by working together to address the big issues of our day. Here are a few ways to get started:

+ Use CQ Drive to zoom wide enough to find a problem you're motivated to jointly address, such as immigration, sexual harassment, poverty, or disaster relief.
+ Apply CQ Knowledge by zooming in on the strengths each faith perspective brings to addressing this cause. For example, Protestants' strength in pragmatism, Muslims' bent toward justice and compassion, and Buddhists' emphasis on internal well-being are all critical components of addressing some of the most pressing causes.
+ Rotate who leads and where you meet together so that you build in an opportunity to learn about each faith community, offering an opportunity to further develop your CQ Knowledge.
+ Don't shame people from your faith community if they don't have the CQ Drive to participate. Not everyone is ready, and some may have reasons why participating in this is too difficult (e.g., past experience of oppression or abuse from leaders from one of the participating faiths).
+ Use CQ Strategy and CQ Action to commit to doing something tangible together, such as welcoming Afghan refugees, and measure the results.

Reverence for the Complexity

When my daughter Emily left home for college, she didn't drink, she believed sex was only for marriage, and she regularly read her Bible and prayed. Less than a year later she said: "I'm not sure what I believe any more. It's hard to accept a book written thousands of years ago by a bunch of men." For years, I had been telling parents, "Be grateful when your kids question their faith. It shows they're thinking it through for themselves." But it's another whole thing when you hear it from your own child.

Emily's waning belief had the potential to become polarizing. I thought back to my conversations with Soo-Jin. Linda and I worked hard to listen, love, and engage with Emily rather than defend and debate. My challenge to Emily was to stay open. Don't substitute one form or propaganda for another. I committed that I would stay open too. While we made plenty of mistakes along the way, we lived up to the challenge. Today, some of our richest conversations are deliberating the issues of life, death, meaning, and the universe and remembering that first and foremost we belong to each other.

ELEVEN

Politics

Intro to sociology. It's a class that Thando, a South African professor at an Atlanta university, has been teaching for ten years. All the other faculty want no part of it. But Thando loves it. Most of the students are eighteen or nineteen years old and experiencing the newfound freedom of American college life. And most of them are voting for the first time. I met Thando just a couple months before the Clinton–Trump election. He had just come from class, where he asked each student to share who they were voting for and why.

There were a couple students who lectured their professor on how inappropriate that question is in the US. Seth, a nineteen-year-old from South Carolina said, "My parents won't even tell me who they're voting for, so I don't think it's right for you to make us share this publicly." Thando was of course familiar with this argument. He's been in the US for twenty years. But he didn't let Seth off the hook. Thando said, "Are you embarrassed to say who you're voting for?" Seth vehemently denied that, but he refused to answer the question based on the principle. Thando is fascinated why Americans are so quick to spout off about politics on social media but reticent to simply answer: "Who are you voting for and why?"

There are enormous challenges associated with marrying across religious lines. But a much bigger issue today is marrying across political divides. Since 2010, 40 percent of US couples married across religions. But only 10 percent married across the political aisle. Similar reluctance exists in other countries, with Brits being the most resistant to marry someone from the opposing party.[1] Political differences surround big ideas like how much government should be involved in our lives, securing our borders, and taxes. But practically speaking, we're politically polarized on everything—Covid, education, abortion, health care, policing, race theories, who to cancel, and the list keeps going and going. In the digital age, all our figured worlds converge in the world of politics. Given the global spotlight on US politics, I'm going to focus primarily on political polarization in the US, but many of these themes emerge in other places too.

The Power of Politics

In 2020 the *New York Times* ran a quiz asking readers to look inside a refrigerator and guess whether it belonged to a Trump or Biden supporter. The food most accurately guessed for Trump refrigerators was Cool Whip, chocolate milk, Velveeta cheese, and yellow mustard. Biden refrigerators had organic miso, yogurt, and a large, open carton of eggs. I took the quiz and I missed some. It turns out there are Trump voters who buy coconut milk, and Biden voters who buy cheap beer. But the quiz revealed how much further our political identities go than our views about the size of government, economics, and immigration.[2]

It's no secret that you're more likely to find Republicans in Evangelical churches and the military, and Democrats in higher education and Silicon Valley. But we don't even like living next to each other. Most of us live in partisan bubbles. In fact, "place" is a better predictor of political beliefs in the US than age, gender, occupation, or even religion. And this is true in many other countries too.

Thando calls this American apartheid. He grew up in Soweto, where months passed without him ever seeing a white person. He tells his students these stories and shows them research that indicates they likely grew up segregated with people who voted the same as their parents. He always has a couple students who deny it, supporting their point with stories about competing political signs in next-door neighbors' yards. But research is on Thando's side. A comprehensive view of voting records shows that most Americans live by people who vote the same as them. This is most evident in large urban areas and rural communities. Democrats in large cities encounter a Republican only 7 percent of the time, and the reverse is true in rural areas. But even in communities where there's a more even mix of political parties, we cluster together in small neighborhoods and streets. Similar results exist in many other countries. Not only do many of us live in echo chambers on social media, but we also primarily chat with neighbors who have the same political views as us.[3]

Liberals are more drawn to communities with good public transit, bookstores, and Whole Foods. Conservatives want to live where they can easily attend church, send kids to schools that teach creation science, and shop at Wal-Mart. Homebuyers see symbols like large American flags or Black Lives Matter signs and implicitly conclude what kind of people live there. If we never interact with people who have different political perspectives, the polarization gets deeper. The result is two very different Americans, some of whom are family members who no longer speak to each other. Social media companies and news networks profit by exploiting this political polarization.

Imagine being on a nonprofit board with a fellow board member who is unapologetically Republican. She talks openly about the importance of limited government and believes socialism is a dangerous idea. Yet she fights for racial equity, LGBTQ+ rights, and gives her time, influence, and money to support underresourced communities. She holds conservative values, but she leaves room for nuance and sounds nothing like the chatter on Fox News. If you're a liberal, could you work with someone like this?

You've probably heard of this board member. But you know her better as the yacht-owning heiress who isn't smart enough to sharpen her own pencils and thinks teachers should have guns in case they encounter grizzly bears. Seeing the way my friend and fellow board member Betsy DeVos, Trump's secretary of education, was portrayed by the media, gave me a first-hand seat in how much we're all being played. Secretary Devos and I have some ideological differences, and we didn't shy away from those when we served together on a board. We both supported organizing forums with rigorous debate about wealth creation versus wealth distribution, and we discussed the issues associated with allowing parents to choose where they send their kids to school. I'm not interested in defending whether Betsy made the right decision in working for Trump. I just know the media showed a very different person than the one I saw up close.

Republicans are the most distrusting of the mainstream media and with good reason. Obama wrote: "I'd gotten to know most of the national political reporters, and on the whole, I found them to be smart, hardworking, ethical, and committed to getting their facts straight. At the same time, conservatives weren't wrong to think that in their personal attitudes, most news reporters fell at the more liberal end of the political spectrum."[4] One study found that 78 percent of US political journalists identify with a political party and of those, eight out of ten are liberal Democrats.[5] On the other hand, how much more mainstream can you get than Fox News? Fox has been the most watched US news source for several years.[6]

Part of the problem is the frenetic, unending competition to give us nonstop news. Life in the digital age means reporters are under constant pressure to meet manic deadlines. The same script is used over and over, whether we're talking about Fox, MSNBC, the *Wall Street Journal*, or the *New York Times*: Report what one side says and include a quick sound bite. Report what the other side says with an opposing sound bite, the more insulting the better. Leave it to an opinion poll to sort out who's right.[7]

A great deal of what gets reported is not news but entertainment for a subset of viewers. Laura Ingraham, Tucker Carlson, Rachel Maddow, and Don Lemon share a little bit of news with a whole lot of personality, commentary, and name calling. We're all being played! Labeling half the nation "country bumpkins" and the other half "global elites" is not reality. But when liberals are repeatedly told that their Republican neighbors are bigots, racists, and white supremacists, and when conservatives are repeatedly told that Democrats are socialists, snowflakes, and immoral demagogues, it begins to seem like fact.

Social media drives an even bigger wedge between us. We curate what facts we read and unfollow anyone with a viewpoint we don't like. It's easy to create an ecosystem where you're rarely exposed to information that challenges what you already believe. When we suddenly find ourselves talking with someone from a different political party, we're not even working from the same set of facts. We live in echo chambers of posting and reposting similar political beliefs where anyone who dissents is quickly shot down. Politics strike at the core of our worst polarization.

Through the Eyes of Politics

Most Americans don't fit the polarized views on display. The largest group of voters are what the Pew Research group calls the Exhausted Majority. They have some strong political ideas, but they think both parties have lost their way. They're exhausted by the growing polarization. They just want to go about their lives without someone shouting at them every minute. This gives me hope.

Eighty-two percent of Americans agree that hate speech is a key problem; but 80 percent also agree that political correctness has gone too far. Sixty-three percent of Americans are concerned that the country's refugee screening process "is not tough enough to keep out possible terrorists," but 64 percent simultaneously believe "people should be able to take refuge."[8] Most Americans are *not* centrists. They have strong opinions on myriad issues, but they're united in their distrust of the government to address the everyday issues of our lives. As we better understand where the key differences lie, we can more effectively address the widening political polarization. For years the dominant political divide surrounded the role of government versus markets. Today, polarization centers as much around globalism versus nationalism. Politicians, family members, and academics debate whether our national borders, neighborhoods, and mind-sets should be open, or whether they should be carefully protected to retain nativist values.

Most students assume Thando, a Black professor teaching sociology, supports throwing open the borders to anyone who wants in. But Thando thinks the conversation will never be addressed as an either/or topic. One day in class, a student asked: "What do you think about Trump referring to your continent as a bunch of shithole countries?" Thando chuckled and said, "Well, yes—many Africans find that offensive. But let's not focus on his latest tweet. Let's look at how he's a mouthpiece for a trend all over the world."

In Trump's speech at the 2016 Republican convention, he said: "Americanism, not globalism, will be our credo."[9] Trump said what a lot of people are thinking, and not just in the US. Thando tells his students that in South Africa there's as much or more animosity toward other African immigrants as there is toward white people. The politicians with momentum across the globe are those who argue that the world is a nasty, threatening place, and that wise nations will build walls to keep it out. These kinds of arguments have secured an ultranationalist government in Hungary and a xenophobic streak in Poland. Populist, authoritarian parties in Europe today enjoy nearly twice as much support as they did in 2000.

The far left reduce the debate to racism and white supremacy, while the far right oversimplify it to security and safety. The Exhausted Majority are left somewhere in between. Most Americans want undocumented immigrants to be treated with dignity and believe asylum should be provided to those in danger. They believe there should be a pathway for citizenship for the children of undocumented immigrants, but they're worried about the state of the US and fear that the American identity is slipping away.[10] Similar sentiments exist among large populations all over the world. Only 18 percent of French believe immigration is good for France. For the average Brit, Brexit was not about economics but about whether to keep letting in immigrants.

I have a hard time seeing how building walls and isolating ourselves plays out in a digital, globalized world. The Covid-19 pandemic was a vivid reminder that we're an interdependent, global world and it takes global solutions and collaboration to address these issues. But neither can we deny that terrorism and fundamentalism are on the rise and communities and nations need to figure out a shared set of guidelines and values to organize how we live together. It can be simultaneously true that immigrants contribute to the economic and human development of our communities and that our nations have the right to regulate if and how immigrants are allowed to come and stay.

Many people I talk to around the world are perplexed why working-class America elected a billionaire who inherited his wealth. *Do they really think Trump is working for them?* Love him or hate him, Trump understood that a lot of people in the US felt left behind by the American Dream. Democratic presidential candidate Andrew Yang couldn't get over the negative reaction he received when he talked with truck drivers, retail workers, and servers in diners across the US and told them he was a Democrat. For Yang, Democrats are the party of the working class. But in the minds of the working-class people he met, Democrats have become coastal, urban elites who are more concerned about policing social issues than improving Americans' way of life that has been declining for years.

The same issue that wreaks havoc on politics in developing countries across the world is the one that has been ripping apart the US, and many political leaders seem to be missing it. Rumbling beneath the debates about racism, gun control, abortion, and same-sex marriage is the more fundamental issue of the haves and have-nots. We need leaders with cultural intelligence who go beneath trending issues to use their CQ Knowledge to understand the key concerns of diverse citizens everywhere.

CQ Solutions

Despite our political polarization, there's reason to be optimistic. For one thing, political views are not held as deeply as religious ones. Only 1 percent of adults change religions, but up to 40 percent shift political views. This is one reason Thando is inspired to keep teaching undergraduates. He's not trying to indoctrinate them; he just wants to be sure they own their views and haven't blindly accepted them. Most Americans are more politically flexible than the extremist groups that get the most media attention. Even if you're a die-hard Republican or Democrat with little flexibility, there are a few scientifically based solutions for how we can narrow the chasm between us. Let's start with how the four cultural intelligence competencies apply, followed by more specific strategies to bridge our political divides.

CQ Drive gives us the motivation to zoom wider than the polarizing sound bites to discover shared concerns that affect all of us, including safety, financial security, education, and health care. With CQ Knowledge, we can better understand what's behind the political perspectives that so easily divide us. For example, liberals would do well to understand the underlying concerns conservatives have with governments mandating vaccines rather than just dismissing everyone as selfish and uneducated. CQ Strategy gives us the tools to manage our confirmation bias, the tendency to look for data and news that supports what we already believe. And it helps us consciously consider viewpoints that are contrary to our default perspectives. CQ Action equips us to use neutral language to describe different political viewpoints rather than resorting to name calling and belittling characterizations.

Let's take these strategies further.

Write a Bigger Story of US

Ronald Reagan and Barack Obama couldn't come from more different backgrounds and political agendas. But both believed that the American miracle was a vision that includes everyone. Reagan said: "You can go to live in France, but you can't become a Frenchman. You can go to live in Germany or Italy, but you can't become a German, an Italian.... But anyone, from any corner of the world, can come to live in the United States and become an American." Barack Obama famously declared: "There's not a black America and white America and Latino America and Asian America; there's the United States of America."

These idealistic sentiments seem worlds apart from the United States we know today. Many Republicans want to narrowly define being an American around language, religion, and merits. Many Democrats think that arguing that there's "not a Black America" sounds dangerously close to "all lives matter." Obama and Reagan galvanized the country by casting a vision bigger than party. We need to rekindle that flame. A total of 77 percent of Americans believe our differences are not so great that we cannot come together. Cultural intelligence never requires agreement about everything. Differences about how to organize our societies have always existed. But we need to reframe our differences as tools to help us address our shared concerns about economic security, equality, and freedom. We have to find some sort of common ground from which to begin crossing the divide.

Covid-19 was a common problem. Rich, poor, liberal, conservative, atheist—we all faced the problem of averting physical, mental, and financial ruin. But so many different worlds focused on who to blame, with political worlds at the forefront of the divides. Whether it's a macro problem like Covid-19, climate change, or economic growth, or more personal issues like how to talk with family members about whether a police officer should be tried for killing a Black man, it's impossible to bridge our different worlds until we agree what the problem is.

Creating a bigger story of us means we have to zoom wider than the sound bites playing across social media (e.g., people resisting arrest versus biased police officers) and get to a core point where we agree (e.g., innocent people shouldn't be shot; we all want to be safe; etc.). Amid all the shouting and name calling lie similar problems shared across many polarized worlds. We must start there.

Let's Talk

Thando doesn't spend much time teaching different political viewpoints in class. Instead, he forces students to talk about political differences with each other. Information without engagement increases polarization. Thando's students complete assignments that require working with classmates who have opposing views. No one is allowed to identify as "undecided" or independent. They must choose a position that is closest to their beliefs. He wants to model the power of interacting with people who disagree with our political opinions.

Thando's students prepare for debates by gathering information with guidance on how to fact-check news sources. These include questions like:

+ What's the source? Check the domain name (e.g., abcnews.com versus abcnews.com.co) and the kind of organization (a partisan or nonpartisan group?).
+ Is this a click-bait headline that has little to do with any verifiable facts in the story?
+ What sources are referenced to back up the claim? If a study is cited, does the study really say what the article claims it says?
+ What's the context? Sometimes a quote is pulled from a couple years prior as if it's addressing something in the current news. Always look for the larger context to understand the meaning.
+ Is it satire? Sites like *The Onion* that are purposely posting fictious, satirical stories are often shared as fact.

+ What's the source of the images? Do a reverse image search and find out where the image came from and whether it's been altered.

Thando insists on the students *talking* through their political differences, not solely making this an intellectual pursuit. Repeated research has shown that direct contact reduces animosity. Anthropologists have used this with opposing tribes all over the world. Washington needs to apply this and so do we.

The Senate Wives Club began during World War I when senators' wives met to knit, sew, and roll bandages to support the troops. After the war their activities expanded to include other charitable work. They continued to meet well into the twentieth century; every week a group of more than fifty women—Democrats, Republicans, and sometimes even the president's wife—sat together in the basement of the Capitol volunteering and exchanging stories about each other's lives. Ellen Proxmire, wife of former Senator William Proxmire said, "We became close friends. We all lived here. We would see each other on weekends."[11]

Times were different then. Most senators moved to Washington with their families and spent evenings and weekends with other senate families. Trent Lott, former senator of Mississippi said: "If you live across the street from your political opponent, if you know his kids, if you've been to dinner at his house, it's impossible to go up on the floor of the Senate or in the media and blast him the next day."[12] Today, it's tough to get elected unless you keep your residence in the community that elected you. Washington is the enemy and dual-family careers make relocating disruptive. When you commute to Washington, bipartisan socializing doesn't rank very high on the list of priorities. We all suffer as a result.

I don't really care where congressional representatives live but the rest of us can use the power of direct contact to chart a different course. Mixed company moderates polarization, like-minded company strengthens it. Thando puts his students in bipartisan groups, and they must argue the opposite of their own political viewpoint. He grades them on how effectively they argue the point of view that is the opposite of their own. It teaches them perspective-taking, which improves their ability to get to the core issues.

Have lunch with people who have different political views, and don't avoid the political discussion. Talk about the differences. This work is emotionally taxing, so do it in small doses. Avoid name calling and see if you can genuinely describe the other view without using demeaning, pejorative language. Broaden your circles of discussion online and debate with others who are at varying points along the political spectrum.

Support Pragmatic Leaders

Thando can't talk about Nelson Mandela without a big grin flashing across his face. What was it about Mandela that forever changed South Africa? Surely he wasn't the first outspoken Black man to challenge the apartheid government. Mandela and Winnie, his wife at the time, were quite the duo. Winnie would rile up the townships by lashing out against the white government. The whole crowd would chant and sing with her. Then Nelson would quietly take the stage and outline the negotiations he was working on with the white rulers. He urged the crowd to exercise self-control.

Mandela had grit, focus, and determination, not the least of which was evidenced by never giving up during twenty-seven years as a political prisoner. The white government offered to release Mandela from prison six times, always with conditions attached. Mandela refused. He balanced vision with compromise and pragmatism. He cast a vision that not only welcomed white people to remain in South Africa but saw them as critical to the nation's future. When elected as president in 1994, he developed policies and structures to support the rainbow nation, creating a place for everyone.

We need pragmatic, visionary leaders in government, education, business, and religion to call us to values and solutions that unify us. Preachers, teachers, and writers can use the power of words to call us back to our shared humanity. Artists can use film, music, and visual arts to highlight communities building bridges. Tech companies can use their platforms to eliminate hate speech and look for innovative ways to facilitate connections across fault lines rather than profiting off amplified outrage. Thriving together in the twenty-first century requires leadership who actively create spaces that connect people across the lines of difference.

A New Kind of Citizen

Political polarization threatens friendship, families, and the very core of society. Unless we can bridge these divisions and forge a new way forward, there's little hope we can address the pressing issues of our day. We must figure out how to not only live together but develop a common vision for a future in which everyone feels like they belong and are respected. It's going to take more than platitudes and political speeches. Our polarization is the consequence of complex economic and social forces that have enduring historical injustices. But vision and idealism are the first step in reclaiming an identity that transcends our political battlegrounds.[13]

As everyday citizens grasp a vision for who we can be together, we can hold our politicians accountable to solve the problems that matter to all of us. We can demonstrate that canceling each other isn't really an option.* And we, the people, can rise above the artificial polarization to build a better world for all of us.

*"Cancel culture" has become another contemporary buzzword that has lost its original meaning. There's enormous history to the power of boycotts as one of the only tools people have to fight against an unjust system. But today's "cancel culture" has become more about shutting off anyone who disagrees with you. That's what I'm arguing against. If we continue down this road of canceling each other, our polarized state of affairs will get progressively worse.

EPILOGUE

All over the world, I see people enjoying some of the same things.

Sunsets

Fishing

Laughing, eating, and talking at a roadside stall or fancy restaurant

Stopping on the street to greet a friend

Sharing a tender moment with a loved one...

We're all just trying to build a safe and meaningful life for ourselves and those we love. It sounds so simple on paper, but it's hard to be a good human. All throughout history we've clustered with others who think and behave like we do. It feels more safe and secure. When it appears someone is threatening our way of life, we draw closer to our in-group and separate from our out-groups. But segregating with like-minded people is no longer realistic or helpful. We're all connected, and there's no going back. As we do the hard work to bridge our divides with cultural intelligence, we can short-circuit the default to polarization and reclaim our shared humanity.

Across numerous studies, examples, and applications, we've discovered how cultural intelligence applies to overcoming polarization. It takes more than just understanding our differences. In our research on cultural intelligence, we repeatedly find that extensive knowledge about cultural differences is valuable (CQ Knowledge), but only when combined with the other CQ competencies (CQ Drive, CQ Strategy, and CQ Action). In fact, if you *only* have a lot of knowledge, you'd actually be better off ignorant, because increased knowledge alone tends to make you overconfident and more likely to manipulate facts to support your point of view. Knowledge needs to be combined with interaction and engagement with the Other, which requires all four CQ competencies. As we move toward one another, we not only overcome ignorance, we can also lead our most fulfilling lives.

Don't cancel each other. Don't call names. Don't avoid the difficult conversations. This isn't just about civility. It's about using our differences to solve problems that matter to all of us. Workable solutions need something from each of us. One of the reasons countries become united during times of war is because we suddenly realize our differences are less important than our survival. But it shouldn't require war and a common enemy to come together.

We're living in an amazing time. We can get from one side of the world to the other in a matter of hours. We can eat dim sum in Edinburgh, crepes in Tokyo, and kimchi tacos in Omaha. We can pursue a degree with peers who come from entirely different worlds. The first couple decades of twenty-first-century technology, travel, and connectivity have fueled polarization. But the next couple decades can be different. Idealistic? Perhaps a little bit, but there are signs of hope all over the place.

Astronauts repeatedly talk about how going to space gives them what psychologists call the "overview effect"—an ability to zoom wider than one's immediate reality and concerns to view humanity and planet Earth as a whole.[1] I hope to have given you a little glimpse of the overview effect. As we put aside our defensive posture and open ourselves to the wildly different worlds surrounding us, we not only transcend polarization, we make new friends and have access to whole new ways of addressing the causes that matter most to us. We need systemic change across organizations, communities, and nations. And systems are created and reinforced by everyday people like you and me.

Start with one conversation with someone from a very different world than yours. Try out these ideas. Argue against your point of view. Ask your counterpart to do the same. Then invite someone else to join your circle. Keep going. And together, we can all strive to be better humans, and make the world a better place for all. After all, you and I pretty much have the same DNA.

QUESTIONS FOR REFLECTION AND DISCUSSION

Part I: Why Can't We All Just Get Along?

1. If you could wave a wand and remove one source of polarization in today's world, what would it be (e.g., political differences, racial injustice, gender inequity, etc.)? Why?
2. How does our shared humanity (99.9 percent the same DNA) affect the way you feel about life in our digital, diverse, and divided world?
3. What figured world/s most strongly shaped your upbringing? To what degree do you still follow the norms of those worlds?
4. With what figured world/s do you feel the greatest sense of connection today?
5. If you could see through the eyes of one other world for a day, what world would you choose? Why?

Part II: Building a More Culturally Intelligent World

6. Evaluating your CQ

+ To what degree are you open and interested in the perspectives and ideas of people who come from very different worlds than you? (CQ Drive)
+ To what degree can you describe the values, norms, and perspectives of other worlds? (CQ Knowledge)
+ To what degree do you anticipate and plan for differences before interacting with someone from a different world? (CQ Strategy)
+ What's your level of flexibility when encountering cultural norms and preferences of other worlds? (CQ Action)

Visit learncq.com to take a CQ Assessment.

7. Talking across the divides
    + Who in your circle of relationships would you like to talk to about a polarizing viewpoint?
    + What is something you and this individual both view as a problem?
    + To what degree can you describe this individual's perspective about the causes and solutions to this problem in neutral terms? Try explaining it in the first-person.

8. Managing differences at work
    + What differences are most challenging for you at work (place, race, gender, functional, age, political, etc.)? Why?
    + What's a common work problem you share with this group?
    + To what degree can you explain this group's perspective on this problem without using evaluative terms? Try explaining it in the first-person.

Part III: CQ Solutions for Polarized Worlds

9. What groups are hardest for you to trust? Why?
10. To what degree did you discuss racial and ethnic differences growing up in your home?
11. To what degree do you reflect the stereotypes for your gender? In what ways are you an anomaly to gender stereotypes in your context?
12. What's your relationship to faith?
13. To what degree do political differences polarize your relationships?

Now What?

14. How has your thinking about your identity changed since beginning this book?
15. Are you hopeful that we can overcome polarization, or does it seem unrealistic and utopian?
16. What idea from the book stands out to you most? How can you use this in your life?
17. What disagreements do you have with the ideas in this book?
18. What lingering questions do you have after reading the book?
19. What's one thing you can do to improve your CQ?
20. What's one conversation you will have in the next two weeks because of reading this book?

NOTES

Chapter 1. Closer Than We Appear

1. Fox News, US Presidential Debate transcript, September 29, 2020, www.usatoday.com/story/news/politics/elections/2020/09/30/presidential-debate-read-full-transcript-first-debate/3587462001/.

2. The Human Genome Project, National Institutes of Health, www.genome.gov/human-genome-project (accessed February 1, 2022).

3. Sonia Shah, *The Next Great Migration* (New York: Bloomsbury Publishing, 2020), 88–89.

4. President Bill Clinton, remarks from June 2000 White House Event, National Institutes of Health, June 26, 2000, www.genome.gov/10001356/june-2000-white-house-event.

5. As paraphrased in Shah, *Next Great Migration*, 88–89.

6. Keno Verseck, "Hungary's Racism Problem," *Spiegel*, November 1, 2013, pp. 2–13, www.spiegel.de/international/europe/hungarian-journalist-says-roma-should-not-be-allowed-to-exist-a-876887.html.

7. As quoted in Amy Chua, *Political Tribes: Group Instinct and the Fate of Nations* (New York: Penguin, 2018), 183.

8. Donald E. Brown, "Human Universals, Human Nature & Human Culture," *Daedalus* 133, no. 4 (2004): 47–54, www.jstor.org/stable/20027944.

9. Catherine Brahic, "Chew on This: Thank Cooking for Your Big Brain," *New Scientist*, July 14, 2010, www.newscientist.com/article/mg20727694-500-chew-on-this-thank-cooking-for-your-big-brain/.

10. As quoted in Bob Holmes and Kate Douglas, "Human Nature: Being

Gossipy," *New Scientist*, April 18, 2012, www.newscientist.com/article/mg21428610-800-human-nature-being-gossipy/.

11. Sean Hannity (host), *The Sean Hannity Show* [TV series episode aired February 5, 2020], Fox News, https://video.foxnews.com/v/6130022889001?playlist_id=5556999982001.

12. N. Kteily, E. Bruneau, A. Waytz, and S. Cotterill, "The Ascent of Man: Theoretical and Empirical Evidence for Blatant Dehumanization," *Journal of Personality and Social Psychology* 109, no. 5 (2015): 901–31.

Chapter 2. Yet We're So Different

1. Alexandra Robbins, *Fraternity: An Inside Look at a Year of Colleges Boys Becoming Men* (New York: Dutton, 2019), 181.

2. Dorothy Holland et al., *Identity and Agency in Cultural Worlds* (Cambridge, MA: Harvard University Press, 1998), 235.

3. B. W. Pelham and M. R. Carvallo, "When Tex and Tess Carpenter Build Houses in Texas: Moderators of Implicit Egotism," *Self and Identity* 14 (2015): 692–723.

4. C. Aberson, M. Healy, and V. Romero, "In-Group Bias and Self Esteem: A Meta-Analysis," Personality and Social Psychology Review, 4, 2000, 157- 173; M.B Brewer, "In-Group Bias in the Minimal Intergroup Situation: A Cognitive-Motivational Analysis," Psychological Bulletin, 86, 1979, 307-324.

5. Xiaoming Jiang, Kira Gossack-Keenan, and Marc D. Pell, "To Believe or Not to Believe? How Voice and Accent Information in Speech Alter Listener Impressions of Trust," *Quarterly Journal of Experimental Psychology* 73, no. 1 (January 2020): 55–79, https://doi.org/10.1177/1747021819865833.

6. M. Sherif, O. J. Harvey, B. J. White, W. R. Hood, and C. W. Sherif, *Intergroup Conflict and Cooperation: The Robbers Cave Experiment*, volume 10 (Norman, OK: University Book Exchange, 1961).

7. Henri Tajfel, "Experiments in Intergroup Discrimination," *Scientific American* 223 (1970): 96–102.

8. Shawn Tully, "Teens: The Most Global Market of All," *Fortune*, May 16, 1994, 90.

9. Seema L. Assefi and Maryanne Garry, "Absolut Memory Distortions: Alcohol Placebos Influence the Misinformation Effect," *Psychological Science* 14, no. 1 (2003): 77–80.

10. *Social and Cultural Aspects of Drinking: A Report to the European Commission* (Oxford, UK: Social Issues Research Centre, 1998), 10–14.

11. Jennifer Eberhardt, *Biased: Uncovering the Hidden Prejudice That Shapes What We See, Think, and Do* (New York: Penguin, 2019), 12.

12. T. Steimer, "The Biology of Fear- and Anxiety-Related Behaviors," *Dialogues in Clinical Neuroscience* 4, no. 3 (2002): 231–49, https://doi.org/10.31887/DCNS.2002.4.3/tsteimer.

13. Eberhardt, *Biased*, 15.

14. Sherif et al., *Intergroup Conflict and Cooperation.*

Chapter 3. And Then There's You

1. I. R. Gizer, K. M. Harrington, and I. D. Waldman, "ADHD: Genetic Influences," in *Encyclopedia of Infant and Early Childhood Development*, edited by B. H. Fiese and M. A. Winter, 12–25 (2008). Cambridge, MA: Elsevier.

2. Arnold Burns, "Proximity and Particularism," *Ethical Perspectives* (October 1996): 157–60.

3. Megan R. Underhill, "Parenting during Ferguson: Making Sense of White Parents' Silence," *Ethnic and Racial Studies* 41, no. 11 (2018): 19–51.

4. C. Miller and B. Vittrup, "The Indirect Effects of Police Racial Bias on African American Families," *Journal of Family Issues* 41, no. 10 (2020): 1699–1722.

5. Philip Zimbardo, *The Time Paradox: The New Psychology of Time That Will Change Your Life* (New York: Free Press, 2008).

6. Kimberlé Williams Crenshaw, "Mapping the Margins: Intersectionality, Identity Politics, and Violence against Women of Color," *Stanford Law Review* 43, no. 6 (1991): 1241–99.

7. Crenshaw, "Mapping the Margins."

Chapter 4. What's Your CQ?

1. J. Sternberg, "A Framework for Understanding Conceptions of Intelligence," in *What Is Intelligence?* edited by R. J. Sternberg and D. K. Detterman, 3–18 (Norwood, NJ: Ablex Publishing, 1986).

2. David Love, "Louis CK and Chris Rock Re-ignite the N Word Debate," CNN, December 25, 2018, www.cnn.com/2018/12/25/opinions/louis-ck-chris-rock-n-word-debate-love/index.html.

3. Thomas Rockstuhl and Linn Van-Dyne, "A Bi-Factor Theory of the Four-Factor Model of Cultural Intelligence: Meta-Analysis and Theoretical Extensions," *Organizational Behavior and Human Decision Processes* 148 (2018): 124–44.

4. Start with Rockstuhl and Van-Dyne, "Bi-Factor Theory," and L. Raver and L. Van Dyne, "Developing Cultural Intelligence," in *The Cambridge Handbook of Workplace Training and Employee Development*, edited by K. G. Brown, 407–44 (Cambridge, UK: Cambridge University Press, 2018).

Chapter 5. How to Navigate Polarizing Conversations

1. Adam G. Galinsky, Joe C. Magee, M. Ena Inesi, and Deborah H. Gruenfield, "Power and Perspectives Not Taken," *Psychological Science* 17 (December 2006): 1068–74.

2. A. D. Galinsky and G. B. Moskowitz, "Perspective-Taking: Decreasing Stereotype Expression, Stereotype Accessibility, and In-Group Favoritism," *Journal of Personality and Social Psychology* 78, no. 4 (2000): 708–24.

3. Jay Shambaugh and Ryan Nunn, "Why Wages Aren't Growing in America," *Harvard Business Review* (October 2017), https://hbr.org/2017/10/why-wages-arent-growing-in-america.

4. Matthew Hornsey, J. Harris, Emily Fielding, and S. Kelly, "The Psychological Roots of Anti-Vaccination Attitudes: A 24-Nation Investigation," *Health Psychology* 37, no. 4 (April 2018): 307–15.

5. John Banas and Stephen Rains, "A Meta-Analysis of Research on Inoculation Theory," *Communication Monographs* 77, no. 3 (2010): 281–311.

6. S. Rubak, A. Sandbaek, T. Lauritzen, and B. Christensen, "Motivational Interviewing: A Systematic Review and Meta-Analysis," *British Journal of General Practice: The Journal of the Royal College of General Practitioners* 55, no. 513 (2005): 305–12.

7. P. M. Fernbach, T. Rogers, C. R. Fox, and S. A. Sloman, "Political Extremism Is Supported by an Illusion of Understanding," *Psychological Science* 24, no. 6 (2013): 939–46.

8. Adam Grant, "The Science of Reasoning with Unreasonable People," *New York Times*, January 31, 2021, www.nytimes.com/2021/01/31/opinion/change-someones-mind.html.

9. Todd Kashdan, *Curious: Discover the Missing Ingredient to a Fulfilling Life* (New York: HarperCollins, 2009).

10. See Adam Grant's book *Think Again* (New York: Viking, 2021) for much more on how to provoke others to engage in critical thinking.

Chapter 6. How to Compete with Robots

1. Sanjay Gupta, *Keep Sharp: Build a Better Brain at Any Age* (New York: Simon & Schuster, 2021), 117.

2. Joseph Aoun, *Robot-Proof: Higher Education in the Age of Artificial Intelligence* (Cambridge, MA: MIT Press, 2017).

3. Matthew Schumacher, Los Angeles Sheriff's Department, personal conversation with the author, March 10, 2020.

4. David Livermore, *Leading with Cultural Intelligence: The Real Secret to Success* (New York: AMACOM, 2014), 126–28.

5. See Livermore, *Leading with Cultural Intelligence*, or Erin Meyer, *The Culture Map* (New York: Public Affairs, 2014).

6. Janine Willis and Alexander Todorov, "First Impressions: Making Up Your Mind after a 100-Ms Exposure to a Face," *Psychological Science* 17 (2006): 592–98.

7. World Economic Forum, *The Future of Jobs Report* (Geneva, Switzerland, October 2020), www3.weforum.org/docs/WEF_Future_of_Jobs_2020.pdf.

8. Erin Meyer, *The Culture Map: Breaking through the Invisible Boundaries of Global Business* (New York: Public Affairs, 2014), 93.

9. David Livermore, *Driven by Difference: How Great Companies Fuel Innovation Through Diversity* (New York: AMACOM, 2016), chapter 1.

10. Art Markman, "How You Define the Problem Determines Whether You Solve It," *Harvard Business Review*, June 8, 2017, https://hbr.org/2017/06/how-you-define-the-problem-determines-whether-you-solve-it.

11. World Economic Forum, *Future of Jobs Report*.

Chapter 7. Place

1. Bruce Stokes, "What It Takes to Truly Be 'One of Us,'" Pew Research Group, February 1, 2017, www.pewresearch.org/global/2017/02/01/what-it-takes-to-truly-be-one-of-us/.

2. Victoria C. Plaut, Hazel Rose Markus, Jodi R. Treadway, and Alyssa S. Fu, "The Cultural Construction of Self and Well-Being: A Tale of Two Cities," *Personality and Social Psychology Bulletin* 38, no. 12 (December 2012): 1644–58.

3. Fenny Ang, "Do I Trust You More If I Think You Are Culturally Intelligent?" (PhD dissertation, University of South Australia, 2012). An investigation on trust-building between expatriate leaders and host country nationals and the role cultural intelligence plays in the trust-building process.

4. Chris Eskine, "Hey y'all. Passengers Don't Trust Pilots with Southern Accents Nearly As Much As Midwestern Pilots," *Los Angeles Times*, September 21, 2018, www.latimes.com/travel/la-tr-airline-pilots-accents-20180921-story.html.

5. Mahzarin Banaji and Anthony Greenwald, *Hidden Biases of Good People* (New York: Delacorte Press, 2013), Kindle edition, Infants section, Loc 1949.

6. William Maddux, Peter H. Kim, Tetsushi Okumura, and Jeanne M. Brett, "Cultural Differences in the Function and Meaning of Apologies," *International Negotiation* 16 (2011): 405–25.

7. Ethan Kross, *Chatter: The Voice in Our Heads, Why It Matters, and How to Harness It* (New York: Crown, 2021), 168–69.

8. Julie Beck, "The Psychology of Home," *The Atlantic*, December 2011, www.theatlantic.com/health/archive/2011/12/the-psychology-of-home-why-where-you-live-means-so-much/249800/.

Chapter 8. Race

1. Luke Willis Thompson, *Autoportrait*, 2017.

2. René Matic, "Luke Willis Thompson's Turner Prize Nomination Is a Blow to Artists of Colour," gal-dem, May 3, 2018, https://gal-dem.com/luke-willis-thompsons-turner-prize-nomination-is-a-blow-to-artists-of-colour/.

3. Niclas Berggren and Therese Nilsson, "Does Economic Freedom Foster Tolerance?" *Kyklos* (Basel) 66, no. 2 (2013): 177–207, https://doi.org/10.1111/kykl.12017.

4. P. Chew, J. Young, and G. Tan, "Racism and the Pinkerton Syndrome in Singapore: Effects of Race on Hiring Decisions," *Journal of Pacific Rim Psychology* 13 (2019): E16, doi:10.1017/prp.2019.9.

5. Alex Stambaugh, "Singapore Advertisement Sparks Brownface Controversy," CNN, July 30, 2019, https://edition.cnn.com/2019/07/30/asia/singapore-brownface-ad-sparks-controversy-intl-hnk-trnd/index.html.

6. Ta-Nehisi Coates, *Between the World and Me* (New York: One World, 2015), 174.

7. Vernellia Randall, "Why Race Matters," Institute on Race, Health Care, and the

Law, University of Dayton, Ohio, January 2021, https://academic.udayton.edu/health/03access/data.htm.

8. Sarah McKinney, *Being White: Stories of Race and Racism* (New York: Routledge, 2004), xviii.

9. McKinney, *Being White*, 21.

10. J. H. Liu and J. László, "Social Representations of History in Malaysia and Singapore," *Asian Journal of Social Psychology* 5 (2002): 3–20.

11. Ibram X. Kendi, *How to Be an Antiracist* (New York: Random House, 2019), 135.

12. Robin DiAngelo, *White Fragility: Why It's So Hard for White People to Talk about Racism* (New York: Penguin, 2019), 31.

13. Charles Horton Cooley, *Human Nature and the Social Order*, revised edition (New York: Charles Scribner's Sons, 1922), 168 (italics added).

14. Austin Channing Brown, *Dear Nice White People* (Substack newsletter), February 17, 2021, https://austinchanning.substack.com/p/dear-nice-white-people/comments#comment-1297906.

15. Gorick Ng, "How to Use Your Privilege to Even the Playing Field," *Harvard Business Review*, July 27, 2021, https://hbr.org/2021/07/how-to-use-your-privilege-to-even-the-playing-field.

16. Amanda Ong, "My Neighbour Murdered Nearly All of My Family, but Now We Are Friends," *The Guardian*, January 12, 2017, www.theguardian.com/world/2017/jan/12/my-neighbour-murdered-my-family-now-we-are-friends-rwanda-genocide.

17. Ong, "My Neighbour Murdered Nearly All of My Family," (italics added).

Chapter 9. Pronouns

1. B. A. Jones, J. Arcelus, W. P. Bouman, and E. Haycraft, "Sport and Transgender People: A Systematic Review of the Literature Relating to Sport Participation and Competitive Sport Policies," *Sports Medicine* 47, no. 4 (2017): 701–16, doi:10.1007/s40279-016-0621-y.

2. Caroline Criado Perez, *Invisible Women: Exposing Data Bias in a World Designed for Me* (New York: Abrams Press, 2019), 50–51.

3. Judith Butler, "Variations on Sex and Gender: Beauvoir's *The Second Sex*," *Yale French Studies* (1986): 172.

4. Julie Bindel, "If We Wanted to Be Straight, We Would Be," *The Guardian*, December 13, 2004, www.theguardian.com/world/2004/dec/14/gayrights.gender.

5. Conversation with the author.

6. Kay Bussey and Albert Bandura, "Social Cognitive Theory of Gender Development and Differentiation," *Psychological Review* 106, no. 4 (1999): 676–713, https://doi.org/10.1037/0033-295X.106.4.676.

7. Darnell Hunt and Ana-Christina Ramón, *2015 Hollywood Diversity Report: Flipping the Script* (Los Angeles, CA: Ralph J. Bunche Center for African American Studies, 2015), 12.

8. Martha Lauzen, *It's a Man's (Celluloid) World: On-Screen Representations of Female*

Characters in the Top 100 Films of 2014 (San Diego: Center for Study of Women and Television, San Diego State University, 2015), 3.

9. Marie Claire-Chappet, "Why Our Obsession with Girl-on-Girl Fights in Reality TV Shows Like *Selling Sunset* and *Real Housewives* Is So Problematic: Are We Tuning in to Unhelpful Female Portrayals?" *Glamour Magazine*, August 10, 2020, www.glamourmagazine.co.uk/article/female-fights-reality-tv.

10. These insights appear in Alexandra Robbins, *Fraternity: An Inside Look at a Year of College Boys Becoming Men* (New York: Penguin, 2019), 170–71.

11. Robbins, *Fraternity*, 278.

12. Busey and Bandura, "Social Cognitive Theory of Gender Development and Differentiation," 676–713.

13. Jules Schroeder, "7 Reasons Why Millennial Men Are Reinventing Masculinity," *Forbes*, October 12, 2017, www.forbes.com/sites/julesschroeder/2017/10/12/the-evolved-man-7-reasons-why-millennial-men-are-reinventing-masculinity/#37e28daa597c.

14. Robbins, *Fraternity*, 272.

15. Justin Baldoni, "Why I'm Done Trying to Be 'Man Enough,'" TED Talk, December 2017, www.ted.com/talks/justin_baldoni_why_i_m_done_trying_to_be_man_enough/transcript#t-14925.

16. Will Hobson, "The Fight for the Future of Transgender Athletes," *Washington Post*, April 15, 2021, www.washingtonpost.com/sports/2021/04/15/transgender-athletes-womens-sports-title-ix/.

17. E. N. Hilton and T. R. Lundberg, "Transgender Women in the Female Category of Sport: Perspectives on Testosterone Suppression and Performance Advantage," *Sports Medicine* 51 (2021): 199–214, https://doi.org/10.1007/s40279-020-01389-3.

18. Sander Hoogendoorn, Hessel Oosterbeek, and Mirjam Van Praag, "The Impact of Gender Diversity on the Performance of Business Teams: Evidence from a Field Experiment," *Management Science* 59, no. 7 (2013): 1514–28.

19. Dorothy Holland et al., *Identity and Agency in Cultural Worlds* (Cambridge, MA: Harvard University Press, 1998), 9–15.

20. Criado Perez, *Invisible Women*.

21. Brad Johnson and David Smith, "Male Allyship Is about Paying Attention," *Harvard Business Review* (February 2021), https://hbr-org.cdn.ampproject.org/c/s/hbr.org/amp/2021/02/male-allyship-is-about-paying-attention.

22. Jacob Poushter, Janell Fetterolf, and Christine Tamir, *A Changing World: Global Views on Diversity, Gender Equality, Family Life, and the Importance of Religion* (Washington, DC: Pew Research Center), April 22, 2019.

Chapter 10. G/god/s

1. Paul Bloom, "Is God an Accident?" *The Atlantic* (December 2005), www.theatlantic.com/magazine/archive/2005/12/is-god-an-accident/304425/.

2. J. H. McKenna, "If You Were Born Elsewhere, You'd Have a Different Religion," *Huffington Post,* March 12, 2017, www.huffpost.com/entry/if-you-were-born-elsewhere-youd-have-a-different_b_58c56cbde4b0c3276fb78630.

3. "The Future of World Religions," Pew Research Center, April 2, 2015, www.pewforum.org/2015/04/02/religious-projections-2010-2050.

4. Alan Wolfe, *The Transformation of American Religion: How We Actually Live Our Faith* (New York: Free Press, 2003), 216.

5. Marsulize Van Niekerk and Gert Breed, "The Role of Parents in the Development of Faith from Birth to Seven Years of Age," *HTS Theological Studies Journal* 74, no. 2 (2018): 56–67.

6. Mark Powell, *What Do They Hear? Bridging the Gap Between Pulpit and Pew* (Nashville, TN: Abingdon, 2007), 11–27.

7. Ramy Youssef, *Fresh Air* interview with Terry Gross, episode airing June 25, 2019, "On Being an 'Allah Carte' Muslim: You Sit in Contradictions," NPR, www.npr.org/2019/06/25/735658229/comic-ramy-youssef-on-being-an-allah-carte-muslim-you-sit-in-contradictions.

8. Caryle Murphy, "Interfaith Marriages Is Common in US, Particularly among the Recently Wed," Pew Research Group, June 2, 2015, www.pewresearch.org/fact-tank/2015/06/02/interfaith-marriage/.

9. Thane Rosenbaum, Book Review: "God Is Not One" by Stephen Prothero, *LA Times*, June 9, 2010, www.latimes.com/archives/la-xpm-2010-jun-09-la-et-book9-20100609-story.html.

10. Stephen Prothero, *God Is Not One: The Eight Rival Religions That Run the World* (New York: HarperOne, 2011).

11. Ranya Idliby, Suzanne Oliver, and Priscilla Warner, *The Faith Club: A Muslim, a Christian, a Jew—Three Women Search for Understanding* (New York: Free Press, 2006).

12. Corporate Religious Equity, Diversity & Inclusion (REDI) Index 2021, Religious Faith and Freedom Foundation, February 9, 2021, https://religiousfreedomandbusiness.org/redi.

13. Eboo Patel, *Acts of Faith: The Story of an American Muslim, the Struggle for the Soul of a Generation* (Boston: Beacon Press, 2007), 14.

14. Kate Shuttleworth, "The Israelis and Palestinians Who Work Together in Peace," *The Guardian*, July 11, 2016, www.theguardian.com/world/2016/jul/11/israel-jews-arabs-palestinians-work-together-peace.

15. Shuttleworth, "Israelis and Palestinians Who Work Together in Peace."

16. Patel, *Acts of Faith*, 168–69.

Chapter 11. Politics

1. Sean Braswell, "Now US Couples Are More Willing to Disagree on Faith Than Politics," *Ozy*, July 10, 2019, www.ozy.com/news-and-politics/are-american-couples-more-willing-to-disagree-on-faith-than-politics/94041/.

2. John Keefe, "Quiz: Can You Tell a 'Trump' Fridge from a 'Biden' Fridge?," *New*

York Times, October 27, 2020, www.nytimes.com/interactive/2020/10/27/upshot/biden-trump-poll-quiz.html.

3. J. R. Brown and R. D. Enos, "The Measurement of Partisan Sorting for 180 Million Voters," *Natural Human Behavior* (2021), https://doi.org/10.1038/s41562-021-01066-z.

4. Barack Obama, *A Promised Land* (New York: Crown, 2020), 259.

5. Hans Hassel, John Holbein, and Matthew Miles, "Journalists May Be Liberal, but This Doesn't Affect Which Candidates They Choose to Cover," *Washington Post*, April 10, 2020, www.washingtonpost.com/politics/2020/04/10/journalists-may-be-liberal-this-doesnt-affect-which-candidates-they-choose-cover/.

6. Mark Jurkowitz, Amy Mitchell, Elisa Shearer, and Mason Walker, "U.S. Media Polarization and the 2020 Election: A Nation Divided," *Journalism*, January 24, 2020, www.journalism.org/2020/01/24/u-s-media-polarization-and-the-2020-election-a-nation-divided/.

7. Obama, *Promised Land.*

8. Stephen Hawkins, Daniel Yudkin, Míriam Juan-Torres, and Tim Dixon, *Hidden Tribes: A Study of America's Polarized Landscape* (New York: More in Common, 2018).

9. "The New Political Divide," *The Economist*, July 30, 2016, www.economist.com/leaders/2016/07/30/the-new-political-divide.

10. Hawkins et al., *Hidden Tribes.*

11. Lisa Miller, "The Commuter Congress," *Newsweek*, January 17, 2011, p. 28.

12. Miller, "Commuter Congress," 29.

13. Hawkins et al., *Hidden Tribes.*

Epilogue

1. D. L. Shapiro, F. White, and B. W. Shackleton, "Overcoming the Tribes Effect: The Overview Effect As a Means to Promote Conflict Resolution," *Peace and Conflict: Journal of Peace Psychology* 25 (2019): 360–63.

ACKNOWLEDGMENTS

It would take another book to fully acknowledge everyone who has contributed to this one. Every book I've written is a collaborative effort, but this one in particular reflects countless voices and contributions from across the world.

My parents immersed me in my first figured worlds. I'm forever grateful for their unconditional love and for having instilled in me the essence of cultural intelligence—living for something bigger than myself and treating people with respect and compassion.

I'm enormously grateful to hundreds of individuals across twenty-five years who have generously participated in the studies I've conducted. Your stories and perspectives have profoundly shaped my understanding of cultural intelligence in real life. And many of you patiently interacted with me again when I followed up with you while writing this book.

I've repeatedly acknowledged that my experience with discrimination and bias is largely theoretical. But many friends and colleagues around the world have helped me fill in the blanks by vulnerably sharing their experiences with me. These include many members of our team at the Cultural Intelligence Center, including Lyla Kohistany, Gonzalo

Ramirez, Shayna Haynes Heard, Sandra Upton, Buhle Dlamini, Ash Sexton, and others.

Soon Ang and Linn Van Dyne, the pioneering researchers of cultural intelligence, come from very different figured worlds than me. But from the very beginning, they've welcomed me as a collaborator and peer. Our friendship and work is one of the greatest gifts of my life.

A diverse cadre of readers offered me early input on a very rough draft of the book. Thank you to Soon Ang, Steve Argue, Lari Bishop, Travis Davis, Rob Dietz, Ellyn Kerr, Emily Livermore, Linda Livermore, Sandra Upton, Ritika Wadwha, Jenny Williams, and Jae Yu. Each of you offered me something different. Initially I was overwhelmed by the amount and diversity of feedback. But you protected me from saying things I didn't intend to say, pushed me to take my ideas further and deeper, and helped me write more clearly.

This is the first book I've published with Berrett-Koehler (BK), and it's been an exceptional experience. Jeevan Sivasubramaniam's interest in the idea from the very beginning caught my attention. You promised me a team at BK who would operate as partners, and you were absolutely right. Every single BK staff member has made me feel like we're publishing this together. Thank you to my editor, Anna Leinberger. You were a true partner from start to finish, offering your editorial expertise, respecting my voice, and contributing your own insights and experiences.

I'd be remiss if I overlooked my publicist Barbara Henricks and her team at Cave Henricks. Thank you for nearly fifteen years of working together. We've been able to do so much good work together and, as usual, you went above and beyond as I wrote this book by sharing your insights well before the book was done. You're an amazing colleague and friend.

To Grace, my youngest daughter whom I affectionately call "Buddy," you keep me from taking life too seriously. I love that you believe so strongly in the issues of justice, equity, and cultural intelligence, but you also know how to help your father take a deep breath, relax, and go find good food. Our shared experiences fill many of these pages, and I love that some of your graphic design does too.

To my firstborn, Emily, you've talked through every iteration of this book with me, but then, that's pretty much how we do everything together. We dialogue, debate, reflect, and dialogue some more. You inspired me to keep going when this pursuit seemed unending. You brainstormed solutions when I felt stuck. And you used your nascent lawyering skills to insist I back up every claim with evidence.

My dearest Linda, what can I say? You're my one and only, my biggest fan, my toughest critic. You live these ideals with me. You've listened to me process every idea of this book on our morning runs, our days "off," our vacations, and our nights out. When I finally let you respond to all my verbal processing, you say just the right thing to bring it all together, which is pretty much what you do in all of life for me.

INDEX

Acting together, 114–116
Affective- vs. neutral-oriented cultures, 71–72
African Americans, 60, 64. *See also* Race
  killings of, 32, 60, 101
"Agree to disagree" approach, 81
Ahmet, 8–11, 13–16
Akifa, 87–90, 94–98
Ally, being an, 130–133
Ang, Soon, 43, 44
Angelenos, 89
Aoun, Joseph, 69
Applications- vs. principles-first cultures, 77–78, 78f
Arguing and listening, 65–66
Atheists, 136–138, 141, 143
Attention bias, 105
Attribution error, fundamental, 25
Autoportrait (film), 101–102
Awareness. *See* CQ Strategy; Racial awareness window; Self-awareness

Baldoni, Justin, 127
Beauvoir, Simone de, 121
Bell, Rob, 119, 122
Bible, 139–140
Biden, Joe, 7, 152
Body parts
  biological sex and, 121
  vs. gender identity, 121
Boston, 89–90
Brainstorming, 96–97
Brazil, 34–36, 92
Brown, Austin Channing, 111–112
Brown, Donald, 12
Brown, Michael, 32

Canada, 29–32

Cancel culture, 163n
Carol, 111, 111f, 112
Castille, Philando, 101–102
Change
  how it should happen, 63–64
  the need for, 133
  what change should happen, 62–63
China, Livermore in, 14, 74, 76
Chinese Singaporeans, 102–103, 106, 112
Chinese workers, 90–91
Christians, 36, 37, 135, 136, 138, 139, 141, 143, 146
Citizen, a new kind of, 163
Closed-mindedness. *See* Open- vs. closed-mindedness
Collectivist vs. individualist orientation, 73, 96–97
Communication
  cultural differences in, 71–73
  neutral, 71
Complexity, reverence for the, 149
Confidence, 65. *See also* CQ Drive
Confirmation bias, 158
Conversation(s)
  mapping, 60
  modulating the temperature of, 66–67
  tense, 109–110
Cooley, Charles Horton, 108
Covid-19 pandemic, 22–23, 81–82, 157, 159
Covid vaccines, 22–23, 64, 81–82
CQ (cultural intelligence), 2. *See also* Cultural Intelligence Center; *specific topics*
  genesis, 42–44
  GPS for a moving destination, 54
  overview and nature of, 39
  polarization and, 165–166
  in real life, 51–54
  research on, 2, 3, 7, 39, 42–44, 49, 61–63, 77, 107, 166
CQ Action (competency), 93, 97, 129, 148, 158
  CQ Drive and, 107, 115
  examples, 131, 144, 146
  and implementing solutions, 83, 86
  overview and nature of, 50–51, 86
  racial groups and, 108
  religion and, 142, 144, 146
CQ certification course, 1, 3, 109
CQ competencies, 44–51, 45f, 53, 56n, 85–86, 142, 158, 166. *See also specific competencies*
CQ Drive (competency), 79, 129, 148
  CQ Action and, 107, 115
  examples, 94, 115, 144
  overview and nature of, 45–47, 56, 85, 93, 158
  racial injustice and, 107–108, 115
  religion and, 142–144
CQ Knowledge (competency), 58, 80, 92–95
  overview and nature of, 47–48, 85
  religion and, 137, 142, 143, 145, 158
  women, gender, inequity, and, 126, 129, 131
CQ Strategy (competency), 93, 95, 108, 148, 158
  confirmation bias and, 158
  gender inequity and, 129

and mapping conversations, 60
overview and nature of, 48–49, 85
problem-solving and, 81
religious differences and, 142
work teams and, 82
Crenshaw, Kimberlé, 11–12, 35, 36
Criado Perez, Caroline, 131
Cross-race effect. *See* Other race effect
Cultural assimilation, 159
Cultural differences, 11. *See also* Racial and ethnic differences; *specific topics*
Cultural intelligence. *See* CQ
Cultural Intelligence Center, 75, 82
Cultural understanding. *See also* CQ Knowledge
understanding their point of view, 58–60
Cultural values, 72–73, 75. *See also* Values
Culturally intelligent problem-solving, 78–84
develop third-way solutions requiring resources and commitment from diverse worlds, 81–83
identify a common problem, 79
implement solutions with the support of leadership and resources, 83–84
understand perceived causes and solutions for the problem, 80–81
Culturally intelligent ways to navigate polarizing conversations, 56
be clear about your goal, 56–58
culturally intelligent dialog, 65–67
map the conservation, 60–64, 61f
take the long view, 67
understand their point of view, 58–60
Curiosity, 142–144

Darwin, Charles, 84
Dehumanization, 10, 16
labels and, 15
N-word and, 47
DeVos, Betsy, 154
Dialogue. *See also specific topics*
across religious lines, 145, 146
culturally intelligent, 65–67
"Different" and "weird," 30, 46–47
Diverse teams, 77, 80, 147
Diversity, 75, 115, 116, 147. *See also specific topics*
develop third-way solutions requiring resources and commitment from diverse worlds, 81–83
intersecting worlds, 34–37
same but different, 16–17
shared problems unite, 24–26
worlds apart, 23–24
"Diversity hires," 107
Diversity programs, 2
DNA, same, 8–11, 21
the 0.1 percent difference, 30–33

Eberhardt, Jennifer, 25
Education. *See* Teachers and teaching
Emily (daughter), 31, 113, 125, 148
Eric, 57, 59, 60, 62–63, 65–67
Expectations, improvising, 93–95

Faith. *See also* Religion
through the eyes of, 139–142
Faith club, forming a, 144–146
Feminist theories vs. frat parties, 124–125
Ferguson protests, 32
Figured worlds, 20, 27, 33, 72, 85, 169
CQ and, 30, 39, 52, 78, 82, 85. *See also specific CQ competencies*
families and, 29, 33
gender and, 96, 121
influence of, 20, 24, 33, 36, 82
interacting with people from different, 24–25, 27, 39, 48, 70
learning about different, 36, 48
politics and, 152
religious faith and, 137, 139, 142
transcending/seeing beyond our, 21, 27
values and, 72
Filipino firm, 87, 90, 94
Filipino women, 36
Finding our way home, 99
First-person perspective-taking, practicing, 66
Flexibility. *See* CQ Action
Floyd, George, 32
Fox News, 59, 60, 154
France, 50
Fraternities and sororities, 19–20, 125
Fundamental attribution error, 25

Galinsky, Adam, 59
Gender
being an ally, 130–133
figured worlds and, 96, 121
mind and, 121
the power of, 120–125
through the eyes of, 126–128
you can go your own way, 129–130
Gender scripts, where we get our, 122
Gender stereotypes, 124, 125, 127
Genetics. *See* Human Genome Project
Golden rule, 11
Google, 37–38
Gossip, 12–13
Grace (daughter), 31, 66, 67, 124
Grant, Adam, 64
"Guardian angel," 113
Gupta, Sanjay, 69
Gyanumaya, 129–130

Hadassah Ein Kerem Hospital, 147
Hayward, Tony, 91
Hijab, 126
Hollywood, 123–124
Human Genome Project (HGP), 9–10, 21
Humanity, degrees of, 14–16

Ice Cube, 47–48
Idliby, Ranya, 144
In-groups and out-groups, 20, 25–27
Inclusion. *See* Transcending differences
India, 34, 90, 106, 133
Individualist vs. collectivist orientation, 73, 96–97
Innovation, 80, 90
Intentions, good, 51

Interest. *See* CQ Drive
Interfaith marriage, 135
Interfaith Youth Core, 147–148
International Olympic Committee (IOC), 128
International Women's Day, 132
Interruption (speech), 71
Intersectionality, 11–12
Islam, 139–141. *See also* Muslims
Islamic clothing, 126
Israeli–Palestinian conflict, 147

Jared, 48, 53–54
Johari window. *See* Racial awareness window
Jonas, 8, 9, 11, 14–16
Judgment, suspending, 49

Katie, 87–88, 90, 92–98
Korean Americans, 138
Kross, Ethan, 98

Labels, 36, 155
  dehumanizing, 15
  losing the, 37–38
  "violent," 70–72
Laurencia, 114
Leaders, supporting pragmatic, 162–163
Leinberger, Anna, 77–78
LGBTQ+ advocates, 122
LGBTQ+ rights
  in Uganda, 41–42, 48–49, 53–54
  US government, Jared, and, 41–42
Linda (wife), 51, 119, 120, 122, 149
Linnaeus, Carl, 10
Listening, 65–66
Logic, 76–77
Long view, taking the, 67
Los Angeles, 71, 89
Lotan, Chaim, 147
Lott, Trent, 161

Maddow, Rachel, 15
Malay Singaporeans, 103, 106
Malena, 52, 53
Mandela, Nelson, 162
Mandela, Winnie, 162
Manorama, Thangjam, 133
Masculinity, 121, 126–127. *See also* Gender
Master status, race as, 104–105
Maya, 33–34
Mbyo, Rwanda, 114, 115, 117
McKinney, Karyn, 106
Media, politics and, 154–155
Medicine, 80–81
Mei, 102–103, 112–114
Melting pot, 159
Mental illness, 71, 80–81
Mental time travel, 98
Meyer, Erin, 77
Muslims, 126, 139–141, 143–146. *See also* Ahmet

N-word, use of the, 47–48
Nationality. *See* Place
Nazra, 102–103, 112
Nepal, 104–105, 129–130
News media, 154
"Nice white people," 111–112
Nooyi, Indra, 133

Obama, Barack, 47, 154, 159
Open- vs. closed-mindedness, 61–62, 65–66
Openness, 142–144. *See also* CQ Drive
Opposites don't attract, 21–23
Other race effect, 25
Overview effect, 166–167

Pari, 102–103
Parker, Doug, 146
Patel, Eboo, 147–148
Perseverance. *See* CQ Drive
Perspective-taking, 58–59, 110f, 162
  practicing first-person, 66
Philippines. *See* Filipino firm
Place, 159
  the power of, 88–90
  through the eyes of, 90–93
Planning. *See* CQ Strategy
Polarizing conversations, 55. *See also* Culturally intelligent ways to navigate polarizing conversations; *specific topics*
Polarizing issues. *See also specific topics*
  how to discuss, 61, 61f
Police violence and race, 32, 60, 101, 104
Politics
  the power of, 152–155
  through the eyes of, 155–158
Pragmatic leaders, supporting, 162–163
Principles- vs. applications-first reasoning, 77–78, 78f
Privilege, 65–67
  redefining, 112–114
Problem(s)
  addressing real, 132–133
  making sense of, 76–78
Problem-solving. *See also* Culturally intelligent problem-solving
  robots helping with, 79
  solving problems together, 95–97
  ways CQ helps solve problems that transcend religious differences, 142–148
Prodigal Son, parable of the, 139–140
Proxmire, Ellen, 161
Puri, 112, 114

Qatar Airways, 72

Race
  polarization and, 101–102
  police violence and, 32, 60, 101, 104
  the power of, 102–105
  through the eyes of, 105–107
Racial and ethnic differences, 8–11
Racial awareness window, 108, 109f–111f, 111
Racial categories, 10
Racism, 10, 55, 101–102. *See also* N-word
  exploiting, 116–117
  police violence and, 32, 101, 104
  reverse, 111–112, 111f
Ramadan, 140, 146
Ramy (Youssef), 141
Reading people, 70–73
Reagan, Ronald, 159
Reasoning, 76–77
  differences in, 76–78, 78f
Relative fundamentalism, 146

Religion, 29–30, 144. *See also* Christians; Faith
  CQ Action and, 142, 144, 146
  CQ Drive and, 142–144
  CQ Knowledge and, 137, 142, 143, 145, 158
  culture and, 139
  curiosity, openness, and, 142–144
  figured worlds and, 137, 139, 142
  the power of, 136–139
Religious differences, 147. *See also* Religious lines/religious divisions
  respecting, 142
  ways CQ competencies help bridge, 142–148
Religious fundamentalism and terrorism, 146
Religious holidays, 140, 146
Religious lines/religious divisions, 29–30, 136. *See also* Religious differences
  dialogue across, 145, 146
  marrying across, 141, 152
  moving across, 138, 142, 158
Resources, access to. *See* Master status
Reynolds, Diamond, 101
Robbers Cave Experiment, 22, 26
Robbins, Alexandra, 125
Robots, 69
  humans behaving/becoming like, 70, 72, 84
  jobs lost to, 84
  limitations, 70, 71, 73, 78, 84
  ways CQ bridges divides in ways robots can't, 70, 76, 78–84
  ways to stand apart from, 73–76
Rosenbaum, Thane, 143
Rwandan genocide, 114, 117

Saito, Kokei (Ko), 34–36
San Francisco, 89–90
Self-awareness, 52, 95. *See also* Racial awareness window
  seeing me through you, 108–112
Self-presentation and, 73–76
Selling Sunset (TV show), 124
Senate Wives Club, 161
Seth, 151
Sexual attraction, 122
Sherif, Muzafer, 22, 26
Silence, 71–72
Similarity attraction, 21
Simon, 19–21, 24
Singapore, 46, 102–103
Singaporeans, 102–103, 106, 112
Skinner, Debra, 129
Socialization, 33–34
Soo-Jin, 135–139, 141, 142, 144, 149
South Korea, 138
Statistics vs. stories, sharing, 64
Stereotypes, 55, 59, 123–127
  Islamic, 14, 15
Steve, 57, 59, 60, 62–63, 65, 66
Stigma, 80–81
Stories vs. statistics, sharing, 64
Sudan and Sudanese, 89, 94–98. *See also* Akifa
Sylvia, 50

Tasian, 114
Teachers and teaching, 1, 52–53, 95, 123, 151, 154, 156

Teams
  diverse, 77, 80, 147. *See also* Diversity
  homogeneous, 77, 80
Terrorism, 37
Terrorists, on a mission together, 146–148
Thando, 151–153, 156, 158, 160–162
Thompson, Luke Willis, 101–102
Time travel, mental, 98
Transcendence and the transcendent, 136, 140, 143
Transcending differences, 27, 81, 97, 142
  transcending religious differences, 142–148
Transgender people, 120, 121, 127–129
  in sports, 120, 127–128
Travis, 45–46
Trump, Donald, 15, 156, 157
  Betsy DeVos and, 154
  vs. Joe Biden, 7, 152
Trust
  cognitive, 90–92
  social, 92–93

Uganda and LGBTQ+, 41–42, 48–49, 53–54
Umar, 23, 24
Universals, human, 11–14

Vaccines, Covid, 22–23, 64, 81–82
Values, 72–73, 75, 89–90, 92–93
Violence. *See also* Police violence and race
  against women, 133
"Violent," labeling people, 70–72

"Weird" and "different," 30, 46–47
Women. *See also* Gender
  violence against, 133
"Wrong"
  admitting that one is, 62
  vs. "different," 30
  listening as if you're, 65–66
  vs. "right," 31
  "weird" and, 30, 47

Yang, Andrew, 157
Young Life, 46
Youssef, Ramy, 140–141
Y2K (Year 2000) problem, 43

ABOUT THE AUTHOR

DAVID LIVERMORE PhD (Michigan State University) is a social scientist devoted to the topics of cultural intelligence (CQ) and global leadership and the author of several award-winning books, including *Leading with Cultural Intelligence*, *Driven by Difference*, and *Serving with Eyes Wide Open*.

David is a founder of the Cultural Intelligence Center in East Lansing, Michigan, and a visiting research fellow at Nanyang Technological University in Singapore. He consults with global organizations around the world, including the Harvard Business School, Google, Coca-Cola, the US Department of Defense, BMW, Qatar Airways, the United Nations, and dozens more. He has traveled to more than one hundred countries and is a frequent speaker at conferences. He also serves on several boards.

David loves to make social science accessible to practitioners. He has been interviewed and referenced by myriad news sources, including *The Atlantic*, CBS News, *Christian Science Monitor*, *The Economist*, *Forbes*,

NBC, the *New York Times, USA Today,* the *Financial Times,* the *Wall Street Journal*, and the *South China Post*.

David and his wife, Linda, have two adult daughters, Emily and Grace. Emily is embarking on a career as a litigation lawyer, and Grace is a graphic designer. Some of their favorite family activities are traveling (fortunately!) and discovering new foods together.

Visit davidlivermore.com

BK **Berrett–Koehler**
Publishers

Berrett-Koehler is an independent publisher dedicated to an ambitious mission: *Connecting people and ideas to create a world that works for all.*

Our publications span many formats, including print, digital, audio, and video. We also offer online resources, training, and gatherings. And we will continue expanding our products and services to advance our mission.

We believe that the solutions to the world's problems will come from all of us, working at all levels: in our society, in our organizations, and in our own lives. Our publications and resources offer pathways to creating a more just, equitable, and sustainable society. They help people make their organizations more humane, democratic, diverse, and effective (and we don't think there's any contradiction there). And they guide people in creating positive change in their own lives and aligning their personal practices with their aspirations for a better world.

And we strive to practice what we preach through what we call "The BK Way." At the core of this approach is *stewardship,* a deep sense of responsibility to administer the company for the benefit of all of our stakeholder groups, including authors, customers, employees, investors, service providers, sales partners, and the communities and environment around us. Everything we do is built around stewardship and our other core values of *quality, partnership, inclusion,* and *sustainability.*

This is why Berrett-Koehler is the first book publishing company to be both a B Corporation (a rigorous certification) and a benefit corporation (a for-profit legal status), which together require us to adhere to the highest standards for corporate, social, and environmental performance. And it is why we have instituted many pioneering practices (which you can learn about at www.bkconnection.com), including the Berrett-Koehler Constitution, the Bill of Rights and Responsibilities for BK Authors, and our unique Author Days.

We are grateful to our readers, authors, and other friends who are supporting our mission. We ask you to share with us examples of how BK publications and resources are making a difference in your lives, organizations, and communities at www.bkconnection.com/impact.

Dear reader,

Thank you for picking up this book and welcome to the worldwide BK community! You're joining a special group of people who have come together to create positive change in their lives, organizations, and communities.

What's BK all about?

Our mission is to connect people and ideas to create a world that works for all.

Why? Our communities, organizations, and lives get bogged down by old paradigms of self-interest, exclusion, hierarchy, and privilege. But we believe that can change. That's why we seek the leading experts on these challenges—and share their actionable ideas with you.

A welcome gift

To help you get started, we'd like to offer you a **free copy** of one of our bestselling ebooks:

www.bkconnection.com/welcome

When you claim your **free ebook**, you'll also be subscribed to our blog.

Our freshest insights

Access the best new tools and ideas for leaders at all levels on our blog at ideas.bkconnection.com.

Sincerely,

Your friends at Berrett-Koehler